If

An anthology of original one-act plays based on a week of asking… **What if?**

Table of Contents:

Nomads Theatre Company Original Readers

A Note From Carol

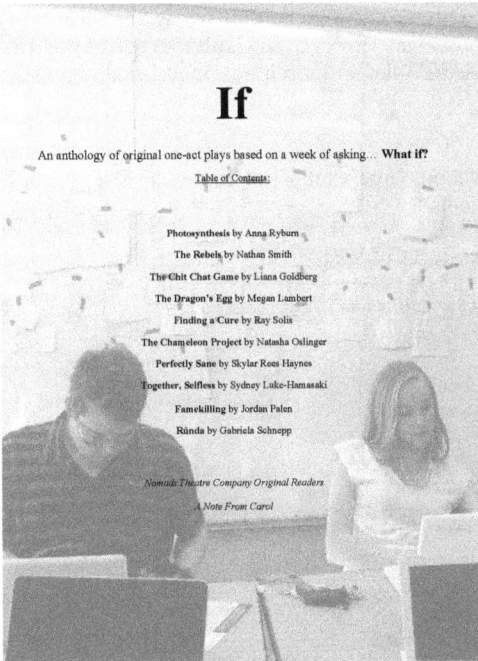

Photosynthesis
by Anna Ryburn

Characters:

LEON: A botanist who acts a bit bizarre. Wants to become known around the world for being the botanist who helped solve serious issues such as illnesses and hunger. He is bitter due to losing his wife to cancer. Deep down, however, he actually deeply cares for and appreciates others, even though he may have strange ways of showing it. He fears that he will die alone and unappreciated.

ASHLEY: Leon's assistant, has a bright mind but is generally quiet and afraid to share ideas. She wants to make a change in the world and get her ideas out there, but fears making mistakes or being criticized. She wants to be respected and appreciated, particularly by Leon, whom she looks up to.

NARISSA: Leon's prized mutant plant that he named after his late wife. It gains intelligence and a human-like body Due to a serum Leon engineered that went horribly wrong.She behaves in a manner that is composed and elegant, almost regal. However, she is also very snarky and has a lot of attitude, especially towards Leon. She sees Ashley as a sort of role model, and wants nothing more than to make her proud.

Setting:

A large, dimly lit greenhouse filled with various large, exotic, and mutant- looking plants. There is a table with pitchers, vials, and other measuring tools.

Scene 1:

At rise, LEON is at the table, working with some of the tools there.

LEON
Ashley! Get in here! I require your assistance!

ASHLEY
What is it?

LEON
Here, stick out your arm.

ASHLEY
Uh... ok?

LEON suddenly jabs a syringe into ASHLEY's arm and pulls back the plunger.

ASHLEY
OW! LEON! What was that for?

LEON turns away and walks over to a table, and begins working with the syringe and vials.

LEON
I needed a sample of your blood. It's for my new version of the serum!

ASHLEY
Couldn't you have taken your own blood instead?

LILLY
Right. Anyways, I've been here for almost a week now, which is a pretty long time, I think. Most people just come for three days at a time. Three day hold or whatever. When are you leaving?

    RAELYN doesn't respond once more

LILLY
… Right. *(long pause)* So are you---

    SETH enters slowly, eyes darting around the new environment. LILLY looks up from the table for a moment, but keeps still until SETH tentatively sits down on the couch. She then bounds over, and hops over the back of the couch, landing in place next to SETH.

SETH
Wh---

LILLY
Hi! You might not want to get comfortable, they're gonna take your shoes.

SETH
What? Why?

LILLY
Shoelaces.

    LILLY does a short gesture, mimicking choking herself with string/shoelaces

SETH
… Oh… I'll just uhm…

    SETH stands, and walks offstage, uncertainty in his step

LILLY
They'll come, you don't have to---

    SETH doesn't return, LILLY sighs, and lays on the couch, staring at the ceiling. RAELYN is in the same position, staring at the radio. Soon enough, SETH enters. LILLY jumps up, and pats the couch next to her.

LILLY
They'd do an exam n' search?

    SETH furrows his brows at her casual demeanor, and slowly sits down.

LILLY
(Chuckling) What? You're not all clammed up like Rae Rae over there, are you?

RAELYN

Perfectly Sane
by Skylar Rees

Characters:
Seth: 15, a regularly quiet boy, Seth is awfully uneager to change and is afraid of medication. He has a loving and supporting family, but his issues are clinical, and lie with his body's inability to produce the proper chemicals to provide emotional stability. He is kindhearted, and willing to examine and understand other things, but ultimately scared of the unknown.
Lilly: 17, a outspoken girl with a very stable set of beliefs. She struggles with addiction, and familial issues, but prefers to cope with her extraverted personality. She is very friendly, but can be witty and snappy when needed.
Raelyn: 16, a very quiet girl, Raelyn prefers to deal with things alone. She suffers from a poor self-image, leading to crippling anorexia. She's taken to wearing sweatshirts and pants in the hospital, and remains silent throughout most conversation. Awfully pessimistic.

Setting:
The main group room of a hospital, a somewhat cozy room, having one couch and a table with a radio, but also has a disturbingly clean feeling.

At rise, LILLY and RAELYN are at the table. RAELYN is sitting in the "corner", but is closer to the audience than LILLY. LILLY is drumming her fingers, and humming lightly.

LILLY
Y'know, it's gonna be awfully boring if we don't talk to each other.

    RAELYN is silent

LILLY
Seriously! Let's talk. It's not like we have to be silent outside of the activities.

    RAELYN remains silent

LILLY
Fine, I'll talk at you. I'll just pretend you're listening or something. I'm Lilly, if you weren't paying attention during the morning group thingymigji--

RAELYN
Morning check in.

LILLY
What?

RAELYN
Morning check in. That's what it's called.

LILLY
Oh, yeah, sorry. Yeah, I'm Lilly, I guess you know why I'm here. If you were paying attention.

    RAELYN does not respond

WILLOW
We need the money.

AIDEN
We can get it another way!

WILLOW
This is the only way to get the amount we need so quickly. You're sick, Aiden. This will pay for the treatment. It's the only way.

AIDEN
If something happens...there is no *me* if there is no *you.*

WILLOW
Nothing will happen. Forming an echo of myself? It all sounds a bit theoretical to me.

AIDEN
But--

WILLOW
I'll be fine, babe, don't worry! You will be there to lead me through it, everything will be okay.

AIDEN
I would hate myself if something happened to you.

WILLOW
(hugging AIDEN) Nothing bad will happen. I promise.

Scene Four
Chairs are returned to where they were, lights are returned to white. WILLOW is lying dead on the middle of the floor. After a few moments of silence, WILLOW stands straight up, face inexpressive, and showing no emotion in her body language. She walks off stage in the same direction AIDEN went.

AIDEN
(Screams)

Lights go out momentarily. Set up is exactly the same as the beginning of scene one, except AIDEN is tied to the chair WILLOW was in and WILLOW is sitting where AIDEN once was, holding a notebook. WILLOW is sitting up straight and shows no emotion.

WILLOW
(In a monotonous voice) What is your name? *(A few seconds of silence)* Ma'am, what is your name?

WILLOW
Why am I here? How did I get here?

AIDEN
I got sick. Do you remember? I got sick…I was going to die. But you wouldn't let me. You volunteered for this. To pay for the hospital bills.

WILLOW
(Trailing off) I-I don't remember when...how did I...

AIDEN
Willow, what does everyone have but no one can lose?

WILLOW
A shadow. *(WILLOW slowly closes her eyes)*

AIDEN
(Lightly slapping WILLOW) Hey, hey, hey stay with me c'mon.

WILLOW
(Mumbling and trailing off) What are you afraid of?

AIDEN
Everything.

WILLOW
Don't be. It's perfect. This is perfect. I'm in your arms….everything is perfect. *(eyes closed)*

AIDEN
(Shaking WILLOW slightly) Willow? Willow!

WILLOW
(In a monotonous voice) One.

AIDEN
(Sobbing and stroking Willows hair) Don't go. Please don't leave me. I'm so sorry. I'm sorry. It's okay. Everything's okay.

Scene Five
Chairs are removed from the scene, AIDEN is standing, she looks weak. WILLOW is standing next to her, the lights are a soft yellow color. They are both wearing different clothes than in the previous scenes.

WILLOW
I'll do it.

AIDEN
No! There is no way, it's way too dangerous! Listen, this project is highly unexplored. Anything could happen.

Trapped in the never space. In the memories that should have been, but never were. Trapped in between being and not being. I see them. I see you. I remember who you are. I remember you now. You're Aiden. I'm Willow. June third. That was going to be the day. Do you remember?

AIDEN
I remember. I could never forget. June third. The day we were going to have our wedding.

WILLOW
I forgot. The memories were gone. What happened to them? Memories of before the Chameleon Project...of you. My memories of you were gone. But their back. I see them...in my head. Like little waves. How could I forget you. My fiancee. Aiden, my fiancee.

AIDEN
Tell me. Tell me what you remember.

WILLOW
The grass. I remember the grass. We were driving and I saw such a beautiful patch of grass. So pretty. Just like you. I made you pull over just so I could sit in it and look at the flowers.

AIDEN
What else? Tell me what else you remember. What do you remember about me. Oh Willow, I'm so sorry, I had to take away the memories so you could complete the experiment. I'm so sorry.

WILLOW
The demons. They sing me lullabies. The demons sing me lullabies and whisper. They tell me things they tell me--

AIDEN
Willow! Focus, what do you remember about me. Keep thinking. Remember.

WILLOW
Our first date. You wanted to go out to dinner. And I wanted to pick up pizza and go through a drive through car wash because I like all the colors of the soap.

AIDEN
Remember which one we did?

WILLOW
They were very pretty colors.

AIDEN
Remember the make your own guacamole bar?

WILLOW
I-I remember! We were gonna hire them for the wedding...but...I can't...I--

AIDEN
Hey, Willow, come on just a couple more minutes.

WILLOW
(In a monotonous voice) Two.

AIDEN
I heard it. *(Silence)* You said two. I know you did. You said three last week. You're counting. What are you counting to?

WILLOW
You, I said you. I've seen you. You're too wonderful to die. I wish I was wonderful. I've seen you in the grass. I remember the grass. Tell me. What happen. Why can't I remember the grass? Remind me.

AIDEN
I will. I promise. I will remind you of the grass. But not yet. You're not ready. Oh, god! We should have stopped earlier...but you're too far. There are only two weeks left. All this week we will finish forcing. I wish you could stop. But you're just too far into the program. If you stop now...you'll...any way. We will wrap up forcing this week, and the next time we meet will be our last. On the 15th, you can stop. We will be done. Everything will be over. Then I will explain the grass. I promise. Everything's gonna be alright.

Lights go out momentarily and WILLOW is lying in AIDENS arms, there is a knife sticking out of her stomach. She is bleeding.

AIDEN
Hey, hey, hey it's okay. Willow it's okay shhh. Look at me, you're going to be okay. What happened?

WILLOW
They did it. The echo. They...they want to settle the score. The shadows settle the score. Don't let it happen. Don't let the marigolds die.

AIDEN
Wil--

WILLOW
There is no such thing as werewolves, Aiden.

AIDEN
Listen to me Willow. I've called an ambulance. They will be here within ten minutes, just...hold on.

WILLOW
Don't fade from me. The wind is calling. Coming dear. Can't you hear me? There is sand in your head! Oh dear!

AIDEN
Hey, look at me...look at me. I won't leave, I'm staying right here.

WILLOW

WILLOW
(Quickly moving away and speaking to someone who isn't there) No. No, don't you touch her.

AIDEN
Willow, who are you talking to?

WILLOW
(Continues talking to no one) She wants to separate us? No. She won't. We are together we will always be together. I won't let them kill the marigolds.

AIDEN
Willow are y--

WILLOW
(In a monotonous voice) Three.

AIDEN
Did you say three?

WILLOW
(To Aiden) Bees. You hear them? Do you hear them buzzing. Buzzing buzz buzz buzz. The bees, the bees in your breath. They sting when we kiss. They corrupt your lungs. *(Turns and continues to talk to no one)* The snakes are crying. Can you hear them? The snakes are screaming and you listen, that's what you do. You listen.

AIDEN
Willow, is the echo in the room? Are they here with us?

WILLOW
Never gone. Nope nope nope. Never gone just out of sight. Like the sun. Never gone, just out of sight.

AIDEN
What are they saying? *(Aiden pulls out the notebook and begins to take notes)*

WILLOW
(Looking back and forth from nothing to Aiden) The light? The unwoven light? Unwoven light is spilling out between your teeth. Telling me to...no. NO! I will not! Don't say that, no! NOT LISTENING CAN'T HEAR YOU NO NO NO! *(Willow covers her ears)*

AIDEN
(Crawls over and uncovers WILLOW ears and holds her hands) Oh, Willow. What have I done to you?

Lights go out momentarily AIDEN and WILLOW are sitting in their chairs.

AIDEN
(Looking at audience) December 8th, 2014.

(Silence for several moments)

WILLOW
(Rocking) The canary is a wolf. You killed the canary, and you made a wolf.

AIDEN
Okay, this has gone far enough, the treatment isn't working. We are stopping the forcing immediately.

WILLOW
NO! No, we can't stop now. I have to keep going. We speak. The echo, I've made the echo, it's--sentient. I can see them...in my head. They're there and I close my eyes and I see them they...lurk. They stand over me when I sleep. I feel them watching. And I hear them...they speak and whisper. Always whisper. Speak louder! I want to hear you, just speak a little louder! Please!

AIDEN
You don't look okay, Willow. I don't care if we have to shut down the experiment. I just need you to be okay. Promise you'll tell me when you stop being okay?

WILLOW
Yes. Yes! I promise! Fine...I'm very fine.

AIDEN
Fine. I'm...I'm just worried what will happen if I push you too far.

Lights go out momentarily AIDEN is kneeling above WILLOW who is curled on the floor and shaking/rocking.

AIDEN
(Looking at audience) December 1st, 2014.

AIDEN *(cont.)*
Willow!

WILLOW
If you love me, you will water the marigolds.

AIDEN
Will--

WILLOW
Slipping away ebbing into the unconscious...the marigolds are dying. They're dying.

AIDEN
Willow, please.

WILLOW
Don't take those pills your boyfriend gave you.

AIDEN
(Holding Willows face in her hands and looking at her) Hey, Willow, look...It's me. It's Aiden. Do you know where you are?

Lights go out momentarily. AIDEN and WILLOW are sitting with their backs pressed together. WILLOW'S head is twitching and shaking every so often. Gradually, WILLOW'S speech becomes more deranged and she begins to act insane.

AIDEN
(Looking at audience) November 24th, 2014.

WILLOW
...That's tastefully offensive.

AIDEN
It's awful!

WILLOW
Well....

AIDEN
Well nothing!

(Several moments of silence then WILLOW turns around to face AIDEN. WILLOW looks puzzled)

AIDEN
Willow?

> *(Silence)*

AIDEN *(cont.)*
Willow are you alright? What's wrong? *(AIDEN moves closer and pulls open WILLOW'S eyelids to see if she is responsive)*

WILLOW
(In a monotonous voice) Four.

AIDEN
Pardon? Willow?

WILLOW
...Before. I said you've said that before. I--I don't...I can't...I--I remember. Grass. I remember the grass. You and me and the grass. Who are you? I know you.

AIDEN
Willow, what do you remember.

WILLOW
Oh, God. What have you done?

AIDEN
Willow!?

WILLOW
No I didn't.

AIDEN
Willow, are you feeling alright?

WILLOW
Fine.

AIDEN
How is forcing going?

WILLOW
How is *what* going?

AIDEN
Forcing. That's what creating an echo is called, because you are *forcing* them into existence. *Forcing.*

WILLOW
Oh. It's...uhh...fine. Something...weird started happening.

AIDEN
(Pulling out a notebook and jotting things down) Like what?

WILLOW
Well...yesterday I was doing my normal forcing routine; 30 minutes of visualization, 30 minutes of vocalized communication, and 30 minutes of internal communication....

AIDEN
And?

WILLOW
And...I got a response.

AIDEN
First external communication! Wow, I have never seen results so quickly! What did they say?

WILLOW
They asked me…if they were alive.

AIDEN
They are, Willow. You created a sentient being. Isn't that amazing?

WILLOW
It's terrifying.

AIDEN
No, I mean. I'm a psychologist.

WILLOW
Are you psychoanalyzing me? Is that what this is all about?

AIDEN
Partially.

WILLOW
Nothing you say ever makes any sense!

AIDEN
Don't worry. Everything will make sense soon.

Lights go out momentarily AIDEN and WILLOW are seated crossed legged on the floor. WILLOW is rocking slightly but noticeably. AIDEN has a book that she is reading out of.

AIDEN
(looking at audience) November 18th, 2014.

AIDEN
(To Willow) Can I continue?

WILLOW
(Laughing) Okay, okay. I'm sorry, please continue.

AIDEN
As I was saying…Poetry for bruised lips: Love is a game of tic tac toe, constantly waiting for the next x or o.

WILLOW
Why are we doing this again?

AIDEN
Because poetry stimulates the mind, and everything will work better if you have a clear head.

WILLOW
(In a monotonous voice) Five.

AIDEN
Pardon?

WILLOW
Fine.

AIDEN
No, you said something else, you said five.

Do you want to stop?

WILLOW
No! Well I don't--I don't care. It's for science. So…

AIDEN
Of course, of course. *Science.*

WILLOW
Don't you start thinking I want to be here. Okay? Because I don't.

AIDEN
Of course.

WILLOW
You look really familiar.

AIDEN
You've seen me before. Remember, yesterday? And the day before that and the day before that. And I will continue to look familiar for the next six weeks.

WILLOW
(Sarcastically) Alright. Whatever you say. Just sayin'…I feel like I know you.

AIDEN
You don't know me.

WILLOW
You don't know me either.

AIDEN
Well, tell me about yourself.

WILLOW
Tell *me* about *yourself.*

AIDEN
God, you are really stubborn.

WILLOW
Se? There's something about me. Now you.

AIEN
Fi I'm not really a scientist.

WOW
I knew it.

studying. They believe a person's 'true personality' differs greatly from the way they actually behave. Having a person and their echo together will show how their personalities differ.

WILLOW
(Several moments of silence) You are completely insane.

AIDEN
Excuse me?

WILLOW
Insane.

AIDEN
I am not!

WILLOW
You are. Now, I listened to your speech. Can I leave?

AIDEN
No. You volunteered for this. You have to do it. Here, you say it's fake? Fine. If in one week you you see no results, then you can leave.

WILLOW
No.

AIDEN
You don't have a choice.

WILLOW
No.

AIDEN
Well you can't leave. So it's either do what I say for a week or you stay tied up here.

　　　　Lights go out momentarily. WILLOW is seated in the same place as before.

AIDEN
(Walks on stage, looking at audience) November 11th, 2014, one week later.

AIDEN (cont.)
(Speaking to WILLOW) How do you feel?

WILLOW
Bored. God this is so dull. Dull! This is really so scientific? Talking to myself. All day everyday sitting in a freezing room trying to "visualize" myself. Trying to think like I would think. How does one think like they think they think? You know what I think? You are trying to drive me crazy. You want to turn me into a mentally unstable vegetable!

AIDEN

AIDEN
There you go. Sleep it off.

WILLOW
Goodnight Flow-man.

Scene 3
WILLOW is strapped to a chair with AIDEN sitting across from her. WILLOW is shaking violently.

AIDEN
(Pulls out notebook and begins taking notes) What are you afraid of?

WILLOW
Everything, okay. Who are you? Where am I? Why am I here and what are you going to do to me! Please let me go. Just let me go, okay? I-I promise I wont tell anyone anything. You don't have to do this, please. What ever your going to do---oh God. Are you...are you going to kill me? Oh I swear to God I will haunt you if you kill me.

AIDEN
I'm not going to kill you.

WILLOW
Oh God, I'm gonna die young! Alone...here. Where ever I am. I want to go home.

AIDEN
Willow, you *have* to calm down. I promise, this will all make sense in a minute. Just calm down.

WILLOW
Fine.

AIDEN
I liked you more when you were tranquilized.

WILLOW
Yeah? I liked me more too. Now explain yourself. Or I'll...I'll start to scream.

AIDEN
You willingly volunteered to undergo a series of tests known as the Chameleon Project. To complete this project, you must lose all memory of the training you have had. This is why you can't remember where you are or how you got here. Over the next seven weeks, you will form an echo of yourself. A echo is a consciousness parallel to your own that is self-aware. It can think, has free will, and has memory. It is developed through interactions and conversations. This version of yourself will have a clean personality slate. To put it in simple terms: throughout your entire life, your personality is shaped depending on who you are around. This is called pragmatic use of language or behavior. You adjust your behavior and use of language based on your perception of the values of the people you encounter. This is not just you. Every ·ingle person in the world does this. It's a natural instinct. This is what the scientists testing on you will be

AIDEN
Pardon?

WILLOW
My name. It's Willow. Like the tree.

AIDEN
Well, Willow like the tree, I'm Aiden. Do you know where you are?

WILLOW
(Laughing) You're pretty.

AIDEN
Do you know where you are, Willow?

WILLOW
Very pretty. Like a flower. But like a human flower. Flow-man. *(Speaks gibberish)*

AIDEN
Pardon?

WILLOW
I'm speaking your native tongue. Flow-man language. *(Continues gibberish)*

AIDEN
In English, please.

WILLOW
I'm in a room. With a pretty flow-man. I don't know where the room is. Maybe Spain. I've always wanted to go to Spain.

    AIDEN pulls out a walkie talkie and speaks into it..

AIDEN
(To walkie talkie) She's still pretty out of it. I need to lower the tranquilizer dosage. She'll sleep it off.

AIDEN *(cont.)*
(To Willow) Alright time for bed.

WILLOW
Nooooooo!

AIDEN
Here we go.

    AIDEN unstraps WILLOW and tries to pull/carry her to the bed in the corner.

WILLOW
(Settling into the bed) Mmmhhh.

AIDEN
The wind.

WILLOW
(Laughter stops) What does everyone have but no one can lose?

AIDEN
(A few seconds of silence) I don't know.

WILLOW
I don't know.

AIDEN
The answer?

WILLOW
The question.

AIDEN
What?

WILLOW
(Mimicking AIDEN) What is your name?

AIDEN
What *is* your name?

WILLOW
My name…is….Kelly.

AIDEN
No it isn't.

WILLOW
No, it isn't, is it? Haha how beautiful!

AIDEN
What is beautiful?

WILLOW
The stars!

AIDEN
You can't see the stars, ma'am, we're inside. Also, its the middle of the day.

WILLOW
Willow.

The Chameleon Project
by Natasha Oslinger

Characters:
Willow: 28, female, strong willed and sarcastic, agreed to undergo the experiments of the Chameleon Project, but had all memory of this and all memory of Aiden erased.
Aiden: 31, female, psychologist that leads Willow through the experiment.

Settings:
Scene 1: A room with two chairs facing eachother and a bed in the corner, all lights are white.
Scene 2: A room with two chairs facing eachother, all lights are white.
Scene 3: A room with two chairs facing eachother, all lights are white.
Scene 4: A room similar to the ones in the previous scenes, except the chairs are removed and the lights are a soft yellow in color.

Scene 1

At rise, Aiden and Willow are sitting across from each other in chairs. Willow's arms and legs are constrained, AIDEN can move freely. Willow is heavily drugged and speaks in a mumbled, delusional way; she sounds drunk. They are both wearing white clothes.

AIDEN
(With a notebook in hand) What is your name? *(A few seconds of silence)* Ma'am, what is your name?

WILLOW
Did you just call me ma'am?

AIDEN
Please state your name.

WILLOW
No one's ever called me ma'am before.

AIDEN
Please sta-

WILLOW
(Laughing) What has teeth, but doesn't bite?

AIDEN
Please answer the question.

WILLOW
I'll answer when you answer.

AIDEN
A comb. Please-

WILLOW
What bites but has no teeth?

(Waits to answer for a moment and she becomes serious) When I was fifteen, I lost my little sister to cancer. I watched her endure months of pain and suffering. It was the worst year of my life. I remember asking the doctors if they could save her. They said they would try. When I asked them to promise me that they would send her back home just like she used to be, they said they couldn't promise me that. I asked them why and they said that there was no way to cure her. *(Begins to cry softly at the memory)* I didn't want to believe it. It was at that moment, that VERY moment, when I swore I would devote the rest of my life to curing cancer and other diseases. I lost my sibling, but I won't let you lose yours.

JASON
(Pauses to take it all in) Holy shit...I'm really sorry about your sister. Please forgive me. I never meant to upset you.

JULIA
No no, it's alright. It's tough for me to deal with even to this day, but I live to save people. I love seeing families and friends brought back together by a cure. Those are the moments I live for.

JASON
Me too.
(JASON looks over at his brother and then back at JULIA)

JASON (cont.)
Do you mind if I take a moment with him before we head to the lab?

JULIA
No problem. Take your time. I'll meet you in the lab when you're ready.

(JULIA exits)

JASON
(Sits right next to his brother's bedside looking at JACKSON'S closed eyes and rests his hand on his shoulder) Jackson, I just wanted to tell you again that I am really sorry this happened. You were right. I should have taken some time off work and maybe we could have spent more time together. Thank you for always being there for me. There is no one else I would have rather taken this journey with. Our journey is not over. This is just a speed bump, but there are so much more we are destined to do together. You will get better, I promise. I'm going to work with Julia on finding a way to cure you. She has a lab across the street where I will be working on developing a medication to heal you. I'll stay there from sunup to sundown if I have to. Julia and I will also be checking on you regularly. I'll do whatever it takes to save you. Hang in there Jackson. I love you.

JACKSON
(Half asleep) I love you too Jason. I believe in you. See you tomorrow.

(JASON exits the hospital room. Lights out)

End of Play

(*Passionately intense*) I propose we create a solution. I say we work together in your lab, day and night until we find a way to cure him. Then once he's better, he and I can bring that same therapy or medication to our other patients from the village.

JULIA
I love the idea, but you don't have any research experience. Do you?

JASON
I don't, but if you teach me, I'm willing to learn. And I am a medical doctor so that should make it somewhat easier. Seriously, I am going to do whatever it takes and I'd love your help.

JULIA
Okay. It's a deal. (*She smiles at him*) You know, I never told you this, but...even though things have been rough lately, I've really enjoyed getting to know you.

JASON
Well, thank you. I've enjoyed getting to know you as well.

JULIA
I mean, I truly admire what you do. All the people you help, it's touching. I've actually always dreamed of working with you someday. You're the reason I got involved in healthcare.

JASON
(*He smiles at her and puts his hand on her shoulder*) You're so sweet. Thank you for everything you're doing to help my brother. I admire you too, and I'm very glad we'll be working together. We'll make a great team!

JULIA
Oh thank you!

(*They hug each other passionately*)

JASON
When can we start in the lab?

JULIA
Right now, if you like. No one's there now, but I think you and I could make wonders happen. And it'll give us a chance to really get to know each other. (*She winks and smiles at him*)

JASON
I love it! (*Pauses for a moment*) Before we go, I wanted to ask you something.

JULIA
Sure. What is it?

JASON
What exactly made you want to go into science?

JULIA

JULIA
I'm really sorry, but unfortunately there is no cure for whatever he has. We're working-

JASON
Shit! Don't tell me that! There has to be something we can do!

JULIA
There is nothing I can give him that won't make it worse. He was injected with a type of poison that seems to be resisting everything I'm already giving him.

JASON
Come on! I'm a doctor and you're a scientist, let's work together here. I can't lose my brother! Please!

JULIA
(*Surprised as she looks over at JACKSON)* Wait a minute, I heard him say something.
(*She walks over to JACKSON)* What was that you said? Can you say that again please? Are you alright?

(*JACKSON moans something that can't be made out clearly.)*

JASON
Jackson, what's wrong?

(*JACKSON speaks more clearly, but still soft*)

JACKSON
Th-thanks...for...being here. (*Coughs*) I-I will not leave you, I promise. You did not leave m-me (*Coughs*) and I can't thank you enough for that.

JASON
You're welcome. You're going to be fine. I'm going to solve this. (*To JULIA*) Julia, how long does he have?

JULIA
All victims respond differently to the poison, so it's hard to tell. Some people die instantly, and others are able to resist for a longer period of time. There isn't enough research yet to know exactly how certain people will respond. He's been holding up pretty well so far though, especially considering how long he's been infected.

JASON
You're right. Some people back in the village who were probably infected with the same poison died right as we got there. Some were still alive when we left. (*Pauses to think for a moment*) Regardless, I'm not going to sit here and watch my own brother die!

JULIA
Well, what do you propose? I'm running out of solutions!

JASON

JULIA (cont.)
Hello? (*pause*) Wait, what's wrong? Oh no! Okay I'll be right in!

Scene 3

At rise, JASON is sitting by his brother's bedside. JULIA is conducting tests on him and reading his monitors.

JASON
What's wrong with him? What the hell did they tell you?

JULIA
Hang on a sec. Don't panic.

JASON
(*Staring at his brother, worried, speaking quietly to him*) Come on buddy, you can make it...you'll be fine. (*To JULIA*) Seriously he's not moving! Please, can you tell me anything? What are you doing?

JULIA
His vitals are not good. The emergency team told me that they are not sure what he is infected with and that's why they sent me in. They aren't scientists, they were just reviving him and setting up additional monitors. Whatever he is infected with, it seems to be attacking his heart and lungs and is spreading throughout his bloodstream.

JASON
What can you do? Please tell me he'll live!

JULIA
Please wait just a little more. Let me check on his other tests.

(*JASON sits by his brother's bedside with one hand on JACKSON'S head and he looks down at the floor, sad and anxious*)

JULIA (cont.)
(*Taps JASON gently on the shoulder*) Jason...I need to talk to you.

JASON
Okay. What's happening?

JULIA
After looking at all of his test results...I'm afraid I don't know what I can do. The infection is impacting his ability to breathe, and our oxygen systems can only help him for a period of time. He is highly infected and my lab and I haven't been able to figure out exactly what he has or how to remove it from his system.

JASON
(*Angry*) Damnit! No no no! Come on! Isn't there something you can give him, a medication, injection, anything at all?

(Pauses to reflect and think to himself and then continues talking to JULIA) We were so close, y'know? We spent our whole lives together. Haha, we both swore we'd become doctors. Not just any doctors though. We dreamed of healing the world.

JULIA
I've heard about the work you both do, traveling to poverty and disease-ridden countries. I've admired you both for years.

JASON
Really? Thank you. That means a lot!

JULIA
I understand what you're going through too. That's why I am a scientist.

JASON
What do you mean?

JULIA
I know how it feels to lose a loved one...so I won't let that happen to you.

JASON
(Pauses briefly) Damn. Thank you very much. I must say I admire your dedication to your work. I'm the same way, only now I feel like my dedication to my work is what brought us into this mess! But, anyway, thank you for your kindness and I'm sorry if I'm on edge.

JULIA
It's ok. I totally get it. I admire your dedication to your work and especially to your brother.

JASON
Thanks. I just wish we could both get through this as soon as possible. *(Pauses for a moment)* I wish I could have a chance to make up for all the time we didn't spend together. He always suggested to me about taking some time off to just enjoy life. Now I don't know if I'll ever get that chance with him.

JULIA
I think you will. I'm going to stop at nothing to help make that happen. If you'd like, maybe you could help me in the lab sometime. You seem like you'd be a great scientist.

JASON
Haha! Thanks, but I'm no scientist.

JULIA
Wrong! You can be anything you want. You are a problem-solver. You help people by healing them. Scientists are problem-solvers who create ways to heal people.

JASON
Well, I don't know. I'll think about it. How-

JULIA
(Interrupts JASON to pick up a call) Excuse me, I need to take this. It's the emergency crew.

JASON
Well, we were in Haiti working with our patients when all of this happened. After all of the deforestation that has occurred though, I don't see how this parasite could exist if they live in that type of environment.

JULIA
They ingest enough nutrients from the ground for them to hunt for their prey. We have found that they primarily target human blood.

JASON
Why human blood? Why not other animals?

JULIA
Human blood contains vitamins and minerals that allow them to mass reproduce.

JASON
Then that would explain why so many people were infected when we were in the village. There must have been millions of those things flying around. I barely saw the one I captured in the tube. It was so tiny. That was pure luck.

JULIA
Well I'm glad you caught one. It will help us find a way to eventually develop a therapy or a cure.

JASON
Is there anything you can give my brother to help him?

JULIA
I don't know. I am going to take a look at his condition after the emergency staff is done.

JASON
What exactly happened to him in there? He was able to talk to me just fine and then he just suddenly stopped moving!

JULIA
From reading his medical report, I believe the infection in his blood caused him to lose consciousness.

JASON
But it seemed like he stopped breathing! Did his heart stop? Is he still alive?

JULIA
Yes. He is still alive. His heart probably just slowed down, but the emergency staff is taking care of that.

JASON
Oh thank God! I just really need him to make it through this.

JULIA
I completely understand.

JASON

JASON

I appreciate that and I get what you're saying, but, I missed out on so many great times we could have had. We used to hang out so much when we were younger. Because of me and my obsession with my work, that is no longer reality and hasn't been for years. And now I can never correct that mistake unless I save you. When you're better, things will be diff--hello? Hey, Jackson? You there? Hey! What's happening to you? HELP! Someone help!

> *JACKSON'S eyes are shut and he is not moving*

Scene 2

At rise, JASON is standing outside of his brother's hospital room, upset, waiting anxiously to talk to his brother's doctor, JULIA, about if and how she can save him. JULIA approaches the entrance where JASON is standing. He stops her to talk to her.

JASON

(Panicking) Excuse me? My brother needs your help immediately! I don't know what's wrong with him. One minute we were talking and then all of a sudden--

JULIA

(Puts her hand on his shoulder) Don't worry. I just received the call about him and I sent in an emergency staff who are caring for him now. I am going to see what's happening for myself as well and I'll see what I can do.

JASON

Oh thank you! Please, if there is anything you can do to save him, try it! Do whatever it takes. I can't lose my brother.

JULIA

I will do everything I can to prevent that, I assure you. My name is Julia and I am your brother's doctor. My lab also received the specimen you sent us.

JASON

Oh, excellent! Wait. You're a scientist? I thought you were a doctor.

JULIA

Yes. I am your brother's doctor and I am also the Principal Investigator of my lab. My team and I are currently conducting a study on the parasite that bit your brother.

JASON

(Shocked, Excited) Oh my God! What have you found? Tell me everything! Can you save him? What was it that bit him? What are the effects? Will it kill him? How do we stop it? Please tell me--

JULIA

(Overwhelmed) Ok! Just wait a second, please. We don't know everything there is to know about it yet. Whatever it is, it has an extremely deadly poison that it injected into his bloodstream. We found reports of infestations in areas abundant with plant life and trees mostly.

Don't you know what happened? They said they had no idea when you'd wake up. I thought I lost you.

JACKSON
What the hell are you talking about? Where are the kids? Were you able to save the little girl?

JASON
We're not in the village anymore. We're back in America at Scripps hospital. At the village, it was pure madness. The place was disease-ridden, more so than ever before. It was tragic. Children were inexplicably dropping dead. Kids lost their parents to sudden fatal illness. People were trying to escape the village, running and screaming in terror for their lives. Some of them leaving mysterious trails of infected blood from their bites. You and I were working frantically trying to get people out of the village and aid those who had been too weak to move. I was trying to save the little girl when you suddenly collapsed. You stopped breathing and I tried to revive you. I sent an emergency signal to our rescue team. They came down instantly and we were flown back to this hospital. When we were in the village, you were bitten by some parasite that came out of nowhere. I think that same type of parasite infested the village earlier this month and that's what caused the epidemic that we got caught in at the village. I don't know for sure, but that's my theory. I talked to some of our colleagues and they believe that when you were bitten, the bug injected you with some type of poison that infected your blood. Nobody knows what that thing even is. We've never seen anything like it. Luckily, I caught one of them in one of my spare medical bottles. I sent it to the lab for inspection and analysis.

JACKSON
Oh...shit! How long was I out?

JASON
A few days. I've been worried sick about you! We should have left the village earlier like you said. I don't know what I was thinking, wanting to stay longer.

JACKSON
No, I get it. You wanted to stay to help people. Don't feel bad. Besides, how could we have known that all of this was going to happen?

JASON
Well, we couldn't. But you were right. I thought I was helping people and what do I get? Almost losing you.

JACKSON
Stop. It's your job to save people. It's OUR job to save people.

JASON
No. I'm not just talking about our experience at the village. I'm saying that I shouldn't have been so focused on my work in general.

JACKSON
You did nothing wrong. You are always there for your patients and I know you're always there for me. I am really sorry this happened but, like I said, we couldn't have prevented it. I will make it through this and we'll have more great times. You'll see.

Finding A Cure
by Ray Solis

Characters:

Jason: 37, a medical doctor who travels around the world with his brother Jackson to give care to the ill in underdeveloped third world countries; too focused on his job; cares about his brother, but doesn't put forth as much effort as he should to build their relationship

Jackson: 36, also a medical doctor; loves the work he does with his brother, but he is more well rounded, wants a balanced life

Julia: 30, a medical doctor and research scientist who is providing medical care for Jackson. Very intelligent and outgoing; wants to connect with and inspire people

Settings:

Scene 1: Hospital room back in America where Jackson is receiving care

Scene 2: Outside of Jackson's hospital room

Scene 3: Back by Jackson's bedside

Scene 1

At rise, JASON is staring with a look of shock, sadness, and hopelessness at his brother JACKSON who is lying ill and unconscious in a hospital bed.

JASON

(*Breathing heavy, concerned*) Jackson? (*pause)* Jackson?! Hey, you there? Come on...please wake up! Please wake up Jackson! Please! Oh God...please help him! How could this happen? Oh who am I kidding?! This is all my fault! I turn my back for one second and---and now it could cost my brother's life. Ugh...what was I thinking? Then again, what could I have done? That little girl was dying! She needed my help. I can't be in two places at once! She needed the injection right then or that would have been the end, and I can't let an innocent child die, especially one who had been alive for just under two short years. I know I did the right thing. I mean, there's no way either I or Jackson could have seen that coming, let alone even known what it was! That vicious pest! So miniscule and puny....yet, so sinister and deadly! It's that little killer's fault, not mine! What on Earth was that thing anyway? I swear...when, not if, but WHEN, I find out exactly what that parasite is, I am going to find a way to wipe them from existence. Maybe that's what's been causing such a huge epidemic in the village! I am almost certain of it! Well, that entire species won't be taking anymore lives if I can help it. And they will NOT be the cause of my brother's death! In fact, I am going to-- (*excited and surprised, JASON gasps*) Jackson! You're alive! Oh thank God! How do you feel?

JACKSON
Wha--Who---are you?

JASON
Jackson, it's ME your brother! You're alive!

JACKSON
Well...of course why wouldn't I be?

JASON

TIFFANY tosses BENEDICT CUMBERBATCH the ring pop.

END OF PLAY

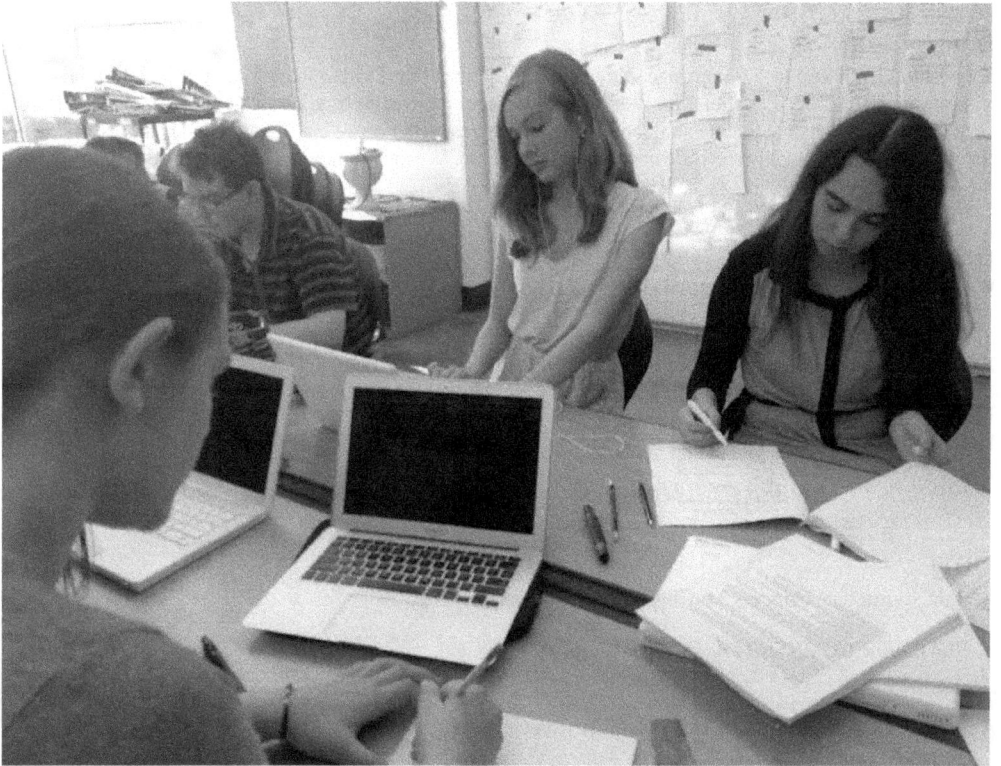

Students work on writing and re-writing in order to get their work prepared in such a short amount of time. This intersession crash course in playwriting had students from 9th, 10th, 11th and 12th grade.

A pause.

TIFFANY
Did your baby sister name it?

TITUS
I'm an only child!!!!

TIFFANY
Okay then...

TITUS
It's best to plan ahead to our marriage. You're just still upset that I killed Leonardo. You'll fall in love with me soon. It's very beneficial for both of us. I will get the wealth of your vast kingdom, and you will have the amazing chance to date someone who actually respects you. We will have lots of kids, to carry on our genetic line. I have a perfect idea for our child's name. We can name our daughter Fluffykins.

BENEDICT CUMBERBATCH's egg cracks.

TITUS
We can name the second one Snowball.

BENEDICT CUMBERBATCH's egg completely falls apart. A small baby dragon's head peaks out. Tiffany is silent, in the background.

TITUS
The third one will be named Kitty Meow Meow. He will be the male heir of our country.

BENEDICT CUMBERBATCH begins to fly out of the incubator. Tiffany notices the BENEDICT, but TITUS is too busy naming child names.

TITUS
And the fourth one, Princess Muffins Fluffyfeet Renaldo.

BENEDICT CUMBERBATCH is right behind TITUS.

TITUS
And the fifth, Princess Earl of Magenta Glitterton Cuteface.

BENEDICT CUMBERBATCH sets his butt on fire. Tiffany stifles a laugh.

BENEDICT CUMBERBATCH
(*In a high-pitched, baby dragon voice*)
I AM FIRE, I AM DEATH!

TITUS lets out a high pitched shriek and falls back onto his butt. He jumps, his butt still on fire, out the window.

No!

TITUS
What?! Say yes!

TIFFANY
No!

TITUS
Yes!

TIFFANY
No.

TITUS
Yes!

TIFFANY
No.

TITUS
Yessssssssssssssssssssssss...

    TITUS begins to sob strangely. He looks more pathetic than saddening.

TITUS (*cont.*)
...sssssssssssssssssssssssssss.

TIFFANY
This is the last time. No. I will not marry you, I do not want to marry you. You will never be my husband.

TITUS
Baby-kins!

TIFFANY
Uh.

TITUS
That is a woman's job! Don't you know? You're supposed to make me pancakes every morning! Have my babies and stuff. Take care of Fluffykins!!!

TIFFANY
Fluffykins?

TITUS
My kitty cat!

TIFFANY
...Fluffykins????????

TITUS
It threatened me

TIFFANY
Exactly how did it do that?

TITUS
It licked me!

TIFFANY
And how is that painful.

TITUS
It is a threat to my manhood!

TIFFANY
Your manhood?

TITUS
I must never appear to be a women. Women are weak.

TIFFANY
(*angry*)
I'm sorry?!

TITUS
Good. You should be. I'm glad you are. You're very rude, you know? You treat men like your play toys. I can't believe you. *I can't believe you.* After all I did for you! You're so inconsiderate. You're so.. despicable. Girls like you are what make guys like me, nice guys, so lonely. We try to do you favors. I got you an egg! I would say that at least warrants me a date. No, a date with a kiss. A date with two kisses! Yes, that's what I deserve. Well, what can I say? Nice guys finish last.

   TIFFANY slaps TITUS.

SCENE 3

At rise, TIFFANY, finally in solitude, begins to read a book. Of course, TITUS is relentless - again, through the window he comes in.

TITUS
This is my final proposal. Marry me or you will never see me again. You will never see me again and no other man in the world will want to marry you. You will be alone, forever.

   A pause.

TITUS (*cont.*)
Well? Will you marry me?

TIFFANY

TIFFANY sighs, and puts the egg in the incubator. Cracks begin to form on the side.

TITUS
Now that I have brought you your egg, Princess...

TITUS gets down on one knee, and takes a Ring-Pop out of pocket. He takes forever to unwrap it. Things start to get a bit awkward.

TITUS (*cont.*)
Will you marry me?

TIFFANY
No!

TITUS
Excuse me. Are you friendzoning me? I'd already set my facebook status as "In a relationship!" After I went out of this way to buy you an egg? I'm hurt. Wounded even.

TIFFANY
You brought me an egg because you killed my dragon.

TITUS
You shouldn't just be flaunting your dragons around.

TIFFANY
What?

TITUS
You're just inviting me to kill it.

TIFFANY
How, exactly?

TITUS
It's just tempting, you know? Can't control these manly urges. I see dragons and I just think, "Wow, I need to kill it." And, just leaving out out there like that... It's not my fault. I just have a lot of testosterone.

TITUS tries to flex his muscles. It doesn't work out very well - he doesn't have many muscles at all.

TIFFANY
Are you... okay?

TITUS
No! I'm upset. Why are you mad at me because of this? I couldn't control it. Dragons are just begging to be killed.

TIFFANY
It was never violent at all! I even got it's fire breathing surgically removed.

TIFFANY
Oh dear god.

TITUS
What of the sweet god?

TIFFANY
Chickens are real.

TITUS
Oh.

TIFFANY
Give me the real egg, Titus.

    TITUS hands TIFFANY the chicken egg.

TIFFANY (*cont.*)
That's the chicken egg, dinghammer.

    TITUS hands TIFFANY the dragon egg.

TIFFANY (*cont.*)
Good. This is the right one.

TITUS
How do you crack it? Do you require a brick to smash it open?

TIFFANY
...

TITUS (*cont.*)
Would you like a brick?

TIFFANY
No. I would *not* like a brick. Dragon eggs require incubators. I still have my old one, though.

TITUS
What will be the dragon's name?

TIFFANY
Benedict Cumberbatch.

TITUS
Cucumberbatch?

TIFFANY
Cumberbatch.

That was another rhetorical question.

TITUS
Oh.

TIFFANY
You can't just buy adult dragons! They have to imprint, you muffin! Leonardo took 10 years to raise properly!

TITUS
I, Miss, can replace any dragon of yours.

TIFFANY
Really?

TITUS
I assure you.

TIFFANY
Go buy me another Dragon Egg, then, Titus. Wal-Mart sells a lot of them.

TITUS
That's... not what I meant.

TIFFANY
Dragon egg. Now. Or I will tell the whole kingdom of your failure.

Scene 2

At rise, TITUS jumps through the window, carrying a cheap dora backpack with two eggs inside. One, a tiny chicken egg. Another, a proper dragon egg. He seems to be confused. TIFFANY waits for him, expectantly.

TITUS
I got two eggs. The customer service guy advised told me to take both of them, he didn't know which one was which either. I think... one of them might appease you, Miss.

TIFFANY
Well, one is a chicken egg.

TITUS
What? It is?

TIFFANY
Yes. Have you never seen a chicken egg before?

TITUS
Are they not creatures of fantasy?

TIFFANY
What can I say? A girl loves her beasts.

TITUS
Miss-

TIFFANY
Why did you kill him? Now he'll never win an Oscar.

TITUS
A *what*?

TIFFANY
Why are you here?

TITUS
I've already said this! I'm here to save you.

TIFFANY
From what? A handsome movie star dragon?

TITUS
You're clearly trapped in here. I, Sir ... Sir Prince Titus Shepard-Smith the Third, am here to save you.

TIFFANY
This is my house.

TITUS
Your house?

TIFFANY
Well, it's certainly not yours. I'd hate to pay for *your* electricity bills.

TITUS
I, uh.

TIFFANY
I can't believe this. You're the third one this week. Do you know how hard it is to raise a dragon?

TITUS
No.

TIFFANY
That was a rhetorical question. Got it?

TITUS
Yes.

TIFFANY

The Dragon's Egg
By Megan Lambert

Characters:
Princess Tiffany. A typical Princess who has lived in a tower all her life. Rather prone to emotion, and a little impulsive.
Prince Titus. A self-proclaimed prince and white knight. Rather inconsiderate and a little bit socially unaware.
Benedict Cumberbatch. A baby dragon, named after one of Tiffany's favorite celebrities.

Setting:
A typical, princess-style tower. Inside it, everything one might need for living - a bed, some lights hanging from the ceiling, a refrigerator. A little messy. There are a few windows letting light in, as well.

Scene 1

TIFFANY sits on her bed, combing her hair calmly. Her peace is disturbed when TITUS jumps in through the window, sword in hand. She looks up, disturbed.

TIFFANY
Excuse me?

TITUS
I have come to save you from your terrible prison. I have spent 7 days and 7 nights laboring hard to defeat the dragon, climb the wall of your tower, and come to your aid. You're welcome.

TIFFANY
You did *what* to the *what?*

TITUS
I killed the dragon. It was a mighty beast, and hard to-

TIFFANY
That was my pet dragon!

   TITUS is quiet in his confusion.

TIFFANY
I can't believe you killed Leonardo DiCaprio!

TITUS
What?

TIFFANY
He was my best friend.

TITUS
You named your dragon Leonardo DiCaprio?

CHAD
I like football because I like to get active and I enjoy to exercise while playing something that I like. Anyways...I am starved. What about you?

SARAH
Me too.

Scene 10
At rise, CHAD taking SARAH home .

CHAD
Well, were here and I see lights on inside...so good night and be safe.

SARAH
I will, thanks... I had a great time

He leans in and then they both kiss

SARAH   *CHAD*

Bye!   Bye!

Scene 11
A rise SARAH opens her snapchat that CHAD sented
SARAH
Oh my God

SARAH sees the snapchat and it was a video that CHAD sented
It is showing that CHAD kissing another girl

SARAH
oh my god!

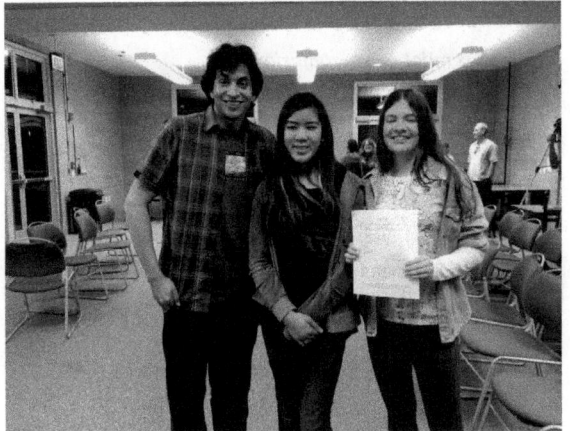

*Liana Goldberg (center)
with original Sarah and
Chad, Elliott Beltran and
Susannah Snowden-Ifft*

The Dragon's Egg
By Megan Lambert

Characters:
Princess Tiffany. A typical Princess who has lived in a tower all her life. Rather prone to emotion, and a little impulsive.
Prince Titus. A self-proclaimed prince and white knight. Rather inconsiderate and a little bit socially unaware.
Benedict Cumberbatch. A baby dragon, named after one of Tiffany's favorite celebrities.

Setting:
A typical, princess-style tower. Inside it, everything one might need for living - a bed, some lights hanging from the ceiling, a refrigerator. A little messy. There are a few windows letting light in, as well.

Scene 1

TIFFANY sits on her bed, combing her hair calmly. Her peace is disturbed when TITUS jumps in through the window, sword in hand. She looks up, disturbed.

TIFFANY
Excuse me?

TITUS
I have come to save you from your terrible prison. I have spent 7 days and 7 nights laboring hard to defeat the dragon, climb the wall of your tower, and come to your aid. You're welcome.

TIFFANY
You did *what* to the *what?*

TITUS
I killed the dragon. It was a mighty beast, and hard to-

TIFFANY
That was my pet dragon!

TITUS is quiet in his confusion.

TIFFANY
I can't believe you killed Leonardo DiCaprio!

TITUS
What?

TIFFANY
He was my best friend.

TITUS
You named your dragon Leonardo DiCaprio?

At rise, at the date at Souplantation

CHAD
Where are you?
(he whispers to himself)

SARAH
Hi!

CHAD
So are you ready to get some dinner? I'm hungry.

SARAH
I am hungry too, and yes I am ready to get dinner.

CHAD
Follow me.

CHAD grabs and then holds SARAH'S hand and walks toward the food. They both got their food and sit at a booth

CHAD
How do you like your soup?

SARAH
It's very good, what about you?

CHAD
Mine is very good too! So what do you like to do for fun?

SARAH
I like shopping for fun!

CHAD
Why do you like to shop?

SARAH
I love to look around the stores and for some reason. I get stressed and I like to treat myself out to get something for myself.

CHAD
Cool, I like playing football and hanging out with my friends.

SARAH
That's cool and seems fun to do. Why do you like it?

So, what are you saying...?

SARAH
We should just be friends..I'm sorry.

CHAD
No, it's okay. We should stay friends and get to know each other even more.

SARAH
Yeah. Things went too fast between us.

SARAH
Friends?

CHAD
Friends!

SARAH
I will see you tomorrow at school.

SCENE 8
At rise, at school at lunch time.

CHAD
Hey, can we talk?

SARAH
Yeah.

CHAD
I don't know what to do because I have feelings for you still.

SARAH
I need to tell you something, I do too.

CHAD
So, are we friends or may I take you on a real date ?

CHAD
Ok, so....it's a date?

SARAH
(she smiles)
Yes, it's a date… wait, when will this be ?

CHAD
How about after school I will meet you at Souplantation.

SARAH
Ok!*(with a smile)*.

Can you hang out tonight? My parents are gone again.

SARAH
Sorry, I have a lot of homework. If I finish, I will call you back and then see if I can.

CHAD
Ok, I will miss you if I don't see you tonight.

SARAH
At least it is Friday and no school tomorrow.

CHAD
Yeah... and can we hang out tomorrow?

      SARAH gets her homework done and calls CHAD back.

SARAH
I got my homework done but my mom is here and I can't get out of the house.

CHAD
Oh...make an excuse to leave or pretend to take out the trash.

SARAH
Ok...anyways I was suppose to put out the trash earlier this morning so I will see you soon.

CHAD
See you soon! Be careful on your way.

Scene 7
At rise, SARAH arrives at CHAD'S house and the doorbell rings and CHAD lets SARAH in.

CHAD
Hey, let's watch some tv!

SARAH
Ok!

    Long pause

CHAD	SARAH
You know about the kiss...	You know, about the kiss?

SARAH
I think it felt awkward since we kissed we haven't really talked with each other like without getting nervous.

CHAD

SARAH
I have to ask you something... is this a date?

CHAD
If you want it to be.

> CHAD looks at SARAH suddenly.... CHAD leans in and they both kiss each other.

CHAD
(with a little smile)
Now it's a date.

Scene 5

> *At Rise, the next day at school at lunch.*

SARAH
I had a fun time last night.

CHAD
(with a smile)
Me too.We should do it again some time.

CHAD *(cont.)*
Well, I got to go to a game and I'll try to win it for you.

SARAH
Aww. thanks!

CHAD
Will you think of me when you are gone? I'll think of you
SARAH
I'll think about you... but you're still here... so I am thinking about you right now.

CHAD
Cool....and see you later.

Scene 6
At rise, both on stage. Later on after school. At both of there houses. SARAH calls CHAD on the phone...suddenly he answers.

CHAD
Hi baby...how are you?

SARAH
Hi!!

CHAD

SARAH*(cont.)*
(she whispers to herself)
Why did I do that?

Scene 3:

AT RISE, that night on Facebook

CHAD
Do you want to come over tonight because my parents are not home? I heard you moved only a few blocks away?

SARAH
Hey. What time should I arrive?

CHAD
7:30pm.

SARAH
But it's 7:28pm now.

CHAD
So then come over now. When you are on your way, I will get a movie ready and make some popcorn that we can share.

SARAH
Ok... I am going to leave right now.

Scene 4

At rise...SARAH arrives at CHAD'S house and rings the doorbell. CHAD let's SARAH in

CHAD
Hi!

SARAH
Hi!

They head to the living room with a movie that just started.

SARAH
What movie?

CHAD
"Titanic."

SARAH
Oh, That's a good movie!!

SARAH and CHAD sit down on the couch and share a bowl of popcorn.

Oh hi, I am good and had a great day. I heard someone saying you're really smart and got an A+ in math. You're so lucky to get that grade.

SARAH
Oh, thanks. I just study a lot which helps me understand the tests that we take.

CHAD
Can I ask you something?

SARAH
Yes. Emoticon smiley face.

CHAD
Do you like me?... Because I see you in class looking at me ....I am just wondering.

SARAH
Maybe a little, but I want to get to know you in person. Why, do you like me?

CHAD
I actually do, but also want to see you and get to know you in person. Well, I'll see you at school tomorrow. Emoticon smiley face.

Scene 2:
At rise, the next day at school, SARAH is talking to her friends from another school on the phone.

SARAH
I was talking to Chad last night. He told me he wanted to get to know me and he said he likes me too, and he mentioned about how I get good grades in class. Also we talked late at night like past ten. I really like him because he seems nice.

   SARAH screams excitedly and then she hangs up the phone.

Then CHAD enters from coming down the hall towards SARAH

CHAD
(talking to SARAH in person)
Hi Sarah, I had a great time talking to you and hope to hang out when you are free.

SARAH
Me too...but I would like to get to know you so, we should hang out . Maybe after school sometime. Well See you tomorrow.

SARAH *(cont.)*
(aside)
Should I hug him goodbye or would that make him feel uncomfortable. But I like him but does he feel the same way?

   Sarah hugs him goodbye

The Chit Chat Game
Liana   by Goldberg

Characters:

Chad: 16, is a player because he wants to date girls and wants to see and find the right girl that he will choose
but he notices he likes Sarah and changes his appearance being a player.

Sarah: 15, a little shy and has delicate feelings but can also be outgoing, and likes to go shopping.

Settings:

Scene 1: At Chad's and Sarah's house, chatting online
Scene 2: At a high school
Scene 3: At Chad's and Sarah's house, chatting online again
Scene 4: Chad's house for the movie date
Scene 5: At school during lunch
Scene 6: At Chad's and Sarah's house, chatting on the phone
Scene 7: Chad's house
scene 8: At lunch at school
scene 9: On a date at Souplantation
scene 10: Taking Sarah home
scene 11:The snapchat cheater

Scene 1

At rise, CHAD and SARAH at their own houses (separate rooms) staring at their computers, showing what they are writing.

SARAH

Hi, my name is Sarah. People say I am quite shy. I like talking to my friends about boys and other stuff. I actually have a crush on a football player named Chad. I am on Facebook right now talking to him, of course chatting privately. I don't know what to do because he hasn't written back for a few minutes. My friend Mikayla says to write to him first, but my other friend Chloe says to let him write me first. I don't know, but I'll wait for a few. I can not stop thinking of him and what he will write and respond to me. I had a dream last night that Chad and I are getting married. People say I have a big imagination and I don't show how I feel. I also get nervous around guys..... "WHAT SHOULD I DO!!!" (*screaming to herself)*

CHAD

"I am Chad, I am the Quarterback" for my school football team. I always hear people talk about me and how I am a player and it is true that I get a lot of girls. The truth is, I just want to find the right girl. I am chatting with a girl named Sarah on facebook. Will she write back? I am wondering what she thinks about me and what she is thinking. It's hard to know what girls think of guys and I don't know if I should write first...Why isn't she writing? Is she waiting for me...I AM SO CONFUSED!!!...I'll just write to her.

SARAH
(on Facebook chatting with CHAD)
Hi, How are you?...How was your day?

CHAD

CARL
Oh great. Now you are calling me a Colthian. STOP CALLING ME NAMES!!

CARL and REX exit the control room to go to the briefing room to plan a strike against the enemy's super weapon.

END OF PLAY

Nathan Smith, playwright of The Rebels, with its original CARL and REX, Edward Delos Reyes and Jet Antonio.

REX
He had help from a smuggler from my home planet Earth.

CARL
Why is your planet even called Earth anyway?

REX
Focus, Carl.

CARL
Sorry, sir. Where were we?

REX
There is a reason why the alliance stole these plans. Can you guess?

CARL
To take control of it and use it for ourselves?

REX
Yes.

CARL
Really?

REX
NO, you fool!! To destroy it!!

CARL
But how? It's massive.

REX
I'll request command to find a weakness.

CARL
And what do you think it is going to be?

REX
I'm not sure. But--

An alarm was heard.

Sounds like it's time for the briefing. Come on, noob.

CARL
Its PRIVATE, sir.

REX
Whatever, Colthian.

REX facepalmed his face and rubbed his face down.

REX
That's not a star, noob. It's a sphere.

CARL
Oooohhh. Is it a space ball?

REX
CARL!!! It may look like a ball. But ITS not. YOU MORON!! IDIOT!! Ugh.

CARL
Okay. Okay. Geez. Calm down.

REX
I am calm. I just don't know if you are ready for this kind of information.

CARL
I'm over qualified.

REX
Oh really. Then do you know who sent you these plans?
CARL
Um...uh. You?

REX
No.

CARL
The general of this base?

REX
NO!

CARL
A robot?

REX
NOO!!

CARL
I don't know then, sir.

REX
It was our general of the army.

CARL
Oh him.

Yes?

ASHLEY
Ferns.

LEON
Ferns! Right.

They each prepare to exit and go back to their work.

LEON
Ashley?

ASHLEY
Yes?

LEON
Would you mind telling me more about that dream you had? At lunch, I mean. I think it might make an interesting story.

ASHLEY
If I can remember any more of it. *(beat)* See you at lunch.

LEON
Bye.

They exit.

END OF PLAY

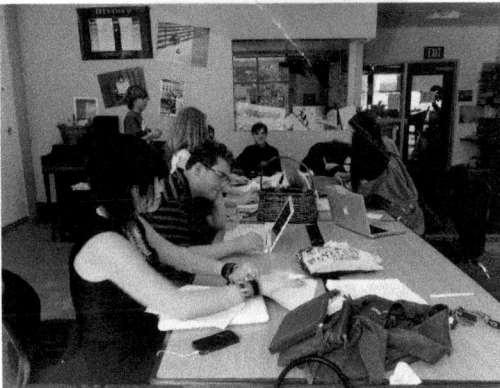

Students work in classroom 129 at High Tech High North County. They were given four days to write one act plays that were read out loud by a college theatre troupe in La Jolla, California.

ASHLEY
Yeah. It was... I think it was so that the serum would be able to work for humans... or something along those lines. Because the whole purpose of it was to give people the ability to photosynthesize.

LEON
Huh... That's actually a really interesting concept.

ASHLEY
Yeah, and so you were making this serum but then we accidentally spilled it onto this rare plant you found in the Amazon that you named after your late wife--

LEON
(with wide eyes) I had a *wife*?

ASHLEY
Yep. So anyway, we spilled the serum with the human blood in it onto this plant, and the next day it had turned into some kind of... plant-woman.

LEON
Plant... woman?

ASHLEY
Her name was Narissa. Or... I guess, that's what your wife's name was... But what am I saying? You named the plant *after* her, so it's the same thing. So, this plant-woman, Narissa, comes to life, and starts talking to us, and she was *really* sassy towards you. She said you talked like your favorite book was the thesaurus... which you actually did, for some reason... I mean, I don't think you literally *read* the thesaurus *like* that, I just mean you talked like that. But anyway, at first you didn't believe she could actually have been a plant. But I did. I mean, it *kinda* made sense. It was the serum we spilled on her. It wasn't an entirely scientific explanation, but it made sense to me. It *was* a dream, after all. But you still weren't buying it. Then, as time went on... I guess she and I together began to convince you. And then she...

LEON
She what?

ASHLEY
She got sick, I guess. The serum *had* side effects. Not only that, *but it* was wearing off, and she was slowly becoming more like a plant again. *And* then she... died.

LEON
Oh.

Another awkward moment of silence.

ASHLEY
Uh... sorry about that. You were right, we're not getting paid to sit around and *chat.*

NARISSA
I'm dying. Right?

ASHLEY does not respond for a moment.

ASHLEY
I'm so sorry. I didn't think the serum would have side effects…

NARISSA
But it's more than that. It's wearing off. *(beat)* That's why my thorns are growing back. That's why I can't move on my own. That's why I--

She freezes again. It lasts longer than before.

ASHLEY
…Narissa?

LEON overhears this and rushes over.

LEON
Narissa?!

NARISSA
--I've been… freezing.

She looks back and forth between LEON and ASHLEY.

NARISSA *(cont.)*
… It happened again, didn't it?

ASHLEY
This is… what? The fifth time now?

LEON
Sixth. *(beat)* It lasted longer, too.

ASHLEY
You're turning back.

NARISSA
(scoffs) I'll be dead before that happens.

LEON
Don't say that!

NARISSA
It's the truth.

ASHLEY

She's right, Leon.

LEON
No! Maybe you just need some more water! A human body requires a lot more energy than you're used to, so if we just--

He grabs the water bottle from ASHLEY and starts pouring it on NARISSA.

ASHLEY
Leon.

LEON
She just needs more water!

ASHLEY
Leon, stop.

LEON
(hysterically) Don't tell me what to do!

He is emptying the contents of the bottle onto her.

NARISSA
Hey.

LEON stares at her.

NARISSA *(cont.)*
I have a mouth, remember?

(She flashes a sad smile.)

LEON
Narissa. Don't leave me. Not again.

NARISSA
You won't be alone. Just let me talk to Ashley for a moment.

LEON hesitates, then walks away.

NARISSA *(cont.)*
I know you'll be there for him. Don't be afraid to talk to him.

ASHLEY
What?

NARISSA
Please, I've been around here long enough to know. *(beat)* You know, you never really spoke to him before I changed.

ASHLEY
But… I talk to him all the time. We work together!

NARISSA
But you never really *spoke* to him, did you? Not until now.

She smiles again.

NARISSA
Promise me this. Don't stop speaking to him. He'll need it. And so do you.

ASHLEY
I promise.

NARISSA
Leon, you can come back now.

LEON returns.

NARISSA *(cont.)*
Goodbye. I enjoyed spending time with you two.

LEON
Narissa, please…

NARISSA
Don't worry about me. I'm okay now.

NARISSA's body stiffens. She closes her eyes.

ASHLEY
She's really gone.

LEON is silent.

Scene 5

At rise, ASHLEY is sitting at a table, face-down and asleep. There are no longer any scientific instruments there. Instead, perhaps, there are some things related to gardening. The greenhouse should look more like a plant nursery than a lab now. LEON enters, carrying a book. When he spots ASHLEY he moves a bit more quietly. Cautiously, he sets the book down and nudges her shoulder.

LEON
…Ashley?

ASHLEY
Mm…? What?

LEON
You didn't go home last night?

ASHLEY
Huh… No, I guess I didn't.

LEON
Working late, I assume?

ASHLEY
(Sarcastically) Nah, I *like* resting on a cold, hard desk. So much more comfortable than a bed.

LEON seems somewhat stunned by this comment.

ASHLEY *(cont.)*
(Beat) Uh… That was meant to be a joke. Sorry.

LEON
(Still a bit confused at first) Oh… Oh! No, no, that's alright! *(chuckles slightly)*

There is a long, awkward silence between the both of them.

LEON *(cont.)*
I think I'll just go… tend to the ferns, okay? The nursery's opening in half an hour, and we're not getting paid to sit around and chat, are we?

ASHLEY
I had an interesting dream last night.

LEON
Oh?

ASHLEY
Yeah. And you were there.

LEON
Oh.

ASHLEY
We were, um… scientists, I think? Well, I was your assistant, anyway.

LEON is looking increasingly uncomfortable.

ASHLEY *(cont.)*
And you were making this serum, and you took some of my blood for it--

LEON
Wait, what?

The Rebels
by Nathan Smith

Characters:
Carl: 23, a tall nerdy private of the army who just got out of the academy who is confused about what a the super weapon is and his captain keeps calling him a noob but he actually is not. He is from the planet Colth.

Rex: 60, the big old captain of the army Carl is in who helps explain what the super weapons as he and Carl look over the plans. He has a mustache and keeps calling Carl a noob because he is in charge. He is from the planet Earth.

Setting(s):
Scene 1: A control room of a spaceship that Carl and Rex were passengers in.

Scene 1
At rise, CARL was at a control panel when a picture popped up on his screen. It was the plans to the enemy super weapon. His captain REX enters the control room to check on what CARL is doing.

REX
What is it, noob? Why are you always wearing a jacket first of all?

CARL turns to the captain to salute.

CARL
First of all, I'm a private. And Second, I'm from planet Colth. Don't you get its name?

REX
The government of that planet should change the name.

CARL
But I like the name.

REX
Whatever. So what's that?

CARL
It seems to be some kind of blueprints, sir.

REX
Blueprints you say?

REX comes to the computer to take a look.

It's the plans to the enemy's super weapon.

CARL
Why does it look like a star, sir?

NARISSA
What?

LEON
There are thorns growing out of your arm.

ASHLEY leans in to get a look.

ASHLEY
Oh my god...

LEON
How long has it been like this?!

NARISSA
I... I don't know!

NARISSA starts pacing around frantically. At one point, she freezes and stays completely still, like a statue.

ASHLEY
Narissa...?

ASHLEY waves her hand in front of NARISSA's face. NARISSA doesn't react for a few moments.

NARISSA
Huh?!

LEON
You froze.

NARISSA
I... did?

She suddenly seems dazed.

NARISSA *(cont.)*
Could I have some more water...?

NARISSA collapses. ASHLEY and LEON rush to her aid.

Scene 4

At rise, NARISSA is curled up back in the pot she was originally inside of. She appears to be very sick and weak. More of her plant features are returning. LEON is standing in the corner of the room, away from her, looking stressed. His demeanor reminds one of a person in an ER waiting room. ASHLEY walks over to NARISSA with a bottle of water.

LEON
Thank you, Narissa. I... got that.

ASHLEY
Seriously though... what are we gonna do about all the other plants? We can't move them to another location, but we apparently can't keep them here either.

NARISSA
How about we just kill them all? I don't like them.

ASHLEY
No!

NARISSA
Fine... I'll just ask Leon. *(to LEON)* Leon?

LEON
No, you can't go kill all the other plants.

> *NARISSA wraps her arms around him and makes a pouty face.*

NARISSA
Please?

> *LEON laughs nervously and starts stroking NARISSA's hair. ASHLEY seems somewhat put off by this display.*

ASHLEY
Um--

LEON
Ashley is right. The other plants are important too.

NARISSA
More important than me?

LEON
Well--
ASHLEY
Ok, you two... that's enough. This is making me uncomfortable.

LEON
Oh. Right, sorry.

> *Embarrassed, LEON pushes NARISSA away. He sees her arm and frowns.*

LEON *(cont.)*
What's this?

My roots are down there!

She points at her feet.

LEON
You have a mouth. You can *drink* the water.

NARISSA stares at him for a moment, processing this. She then grabs the spray bottle, unscrews the top, and starts gulping down the water. Once LEON is sure that she's preoccupied, he walks over to ASHLEY.

ASHLEY
(whispering) Okay, can I just be the first to say that this *may* have been a mistake?

LEON
(grinning) Are you kidding? This is fascinating!

ASHLEY
She's killing all the other plants.

LEON
But we may be the first people in the world to learn how plants would behave as sentient beings! With bodies that are actually able to move on their own! Sure, she's attacking the other plants, but isn't the sacrifice worth taking? Besides, she just thinks they're taking up too much space.

ASHLEY
Well, what if she decides *you're* taking up too much space?

LEON suddenly looks worried. NARISSA, who has finished drinking the water, walks over.

NARISSA
So long as you keep feeding me, you should be safe.

LEON continues to look worried.

NARISSA *(cont.)*
I was joking. That was a joke. You humans do that, don't you?

ASHLEY
Oh, so you *are* gonna kill him, regardless of what he does?

LEON
Hey!

ASHLEY and NARISSA exchange looks and start laughing.

ASHLEY
You should see the look on your face.

NARISSA
(still laughing) You see, she was *also* joking!

No, wait! Not what I meant either. It's just… you're usually so quiet. You know? You don't… share what you're thinking. Your ideas. But now, suddenly… You seem like a real leader.

ASHLEY
Oh. Well, thanks.

LEON
And you're right. We should go talk to… the plant-woman.

ASHLEY
(correcting him) Narissa.

LEON
Sure.

They walk back over to NARISSA. End of scene.

Scene 3

At rise, some of the greenhouse's plants are knocked over and appear to be dying. NARISSA is walking around, pulling the leaves off of plants or scratching them with her thorn-nails. ASHLEY is frantically following her around, wringing her hands nervously, perhaps occasionally re-setting an overturned pot or tending to other plants attacked by NARISSA.

ASHLEY
No, come on, let's not--

NARISSA
I told you, I can't live here with all these other plants around me! I feel crowded!

ASHLEY
Leon, what is this?! Why is she doing this?!

LEON enters with a spray bottle.

LEON
Narissa is a very invasive species! She'll kill any other plant within close range if she feels they are limiting her resources!

He sprays NARISSA in the face with the spray bottle.

ASHLEY
What-- She's not a cat!

LEON
But if she's provided with ample nutrients, she may no longer feel the need to destroy other plants!

He sprays her face again.

NARISSA

LEON
I'm just trying to listen to reason here!

ASHLEY
And so am I! Just listen to what she's saying. *(short pause as ASHLEY thinks)* For example, how could she have known that you found her in the Amazon like you did?

LEON
Well I don't know, maybe she's been keeping tabs on me somehow? Would you find it that surprising that someone might want to steal our research? It would also explain why Narissa is gone!

NARISSA
(from the other side of the room) I've told you, I'm right here!

ASHLEY
Really? If she wanted to steal from us, I don't think she'd do it by dressing herself up as a plant. The same plant, I might add, that she supposedly wants to steal!

LEON
I don't know why she would do it, I just can't bring myself to believe the alternative!

ASHLEY
Ok… I think you need to calm down for a--

LEON
What?! Ash--

ASHLEY
Just *calm down*. Let's go and talk to her. I don't entirely believe this either, but I think we should just play along for now. Get her to talk. Got it?

LEON does not respond.

ASHLEY *(cont.)*
What?

LEON
You never talk like that.

ASHLEY
Excuse me?

LEON
Uh… no, I should rephrase that. You're just being so… stubborn?

ASHLEY looks offended.

LEON *(cont.)*

You think this is a joke? Tell me where you've taken my specimen!

ASHLEY
Uh, Leon--

NARISSA
(to LEON. She opens her arms as a way of gesturing at herself) Your plant is right here. Don't you recognise me? You discovered my species. You named me after your late wife.

LEON
Stop that!

ASHLEY
Leon--

NARISSA
You know it's true. I can read it in your face. I've gotten good at that ever since you took me from my forest--

LEON
You are NOT a plant!

> *LEON is trembling. Whether with rage or fear is unknown.*

ASHLEY
Leon!

NARISSA
I think your friend would like to talk to you.

LEON
(to ASHLEY, as though he had forgotten she was there.) Er... sorry. What is it?

ASHLEY
How about we go talk about this for a second?

> *LEON nods and walks to the other end of the room with ASHLEY.*

LEON
You can't honestly believe what that woman says!

ASHLEY
Normally, I would have to agree with you on that. But... I just can't see any other explanation.

LEON
I can! She's dressed herself up like some kind of... plant-woman, and she's playing a sick joke on us!

ASHLEY
Did you see what she looks like? You can't do that with just makeup.

LEON
What-- 'Doesn't it?' ? That's all you have to say? No explanation whatsoever? How do you expect
me to believe you... whatever you are?

NARISSA
I suppose I don't expect you to believe anything, no matter how obvious it may be.

LEON
(stuttering)
I-- what did-- how did you--

ASHLEY
It's the serum, right?

(Beat)

ASHLEY *(cont.)*
What turned you human, I mean.

NARISSA
I'm glad that you were able to guess so quickly, and not let skepticism get in the way of your ideas
like some *other* people.

ASHLEY
Uh... thanks, I guess?

LEON
(clearly still in shock from the absurdity of the whole situation) What-- how... Ashley?

NARISSA
(to LEON) For a man who talks as though his favorite book is the thesaurus, you seem to be short on
words.

   ASHLEY can't help but snicker at this. LEON silences her with a glare.

LEON
Wait... we've only just met. How can you know how I talk?

NARISSA
(condescendingly) Perhaps I'm just very observant.

LEON
Look, *miss*, I don't know what sort of twisted prank this is, but you'd better start explaining yourself
before I call the police.

NARISSA
Look at that. Someone's finally talking like a human being.

LEON

LEON
What?

He looks up at the usual spot of the plant, noticing for the first time that it is missing.

LEON
No. NO!!

ASHLEY
Do you think someone might have taken it?

LEON
I… I don't know… Narissa was pretty valuable. It was the only one I could use for my serum. And I don't know if I can get another… Oh god…

There is commotion somewhere near the back of the room.

LEON *(cont.)*
Who's there? Stop, thief!

He freezes as a strange looking woman stands up.
She has features that look like those of a plant. Specifically, Narissa, the plant.
Her fingernails resemble the rare plant's brightly colored, venomous thorns.

LEON *(cont.)*
Who are you? WHAT are you?

ASHLEY
Leon, she looks like --

NARISSA
(in a smooth but somewhat monotone voice.)
I am *monstera narissia*. You named me when you first discovered me in the Amazon. But I believe you know me better as just 'Narissa', yes?

She attempts a smile. She doesn't do a very good job.

LEON
Are you actually suggesting what I think you're suggesting?

NARISSA
That would depend on what you think I'm suggesting.

LEON
That you are a plant. A plant that turned human, which just… doesn't seem possible.

NARISSA
Doesn't it?

LEON
Don't fret, my dear. A good scientist always expects to run multiple tests. And besides, it wasn't really your fault alone, now was it?

He smiles reassuringly.

ASHLEY
I guess so... but what about that plant? Aren't you worried it might be harmed by the chemicals? That's the species you found in the Amazon. The one named after your... wife...

Her voice trails off. She has brought up a touchy subject for Leon. Leon frowns.

LEON
I suppose you have a point there... but Narissa is pretty tough. However, we'll have to check on her regularly for the next couple weeks or so. Just in case.

He checks the time.

LEON *(cont.)*
It's getting pretty late. I say we both call it a night, and we can resume testing tomorrow. If it bothers you that much, I may be able to find someone else to provide blood for the experiment, okay?

ASHLEY
Alright. See you tomorrow, then.

LEON
Goodnight.

They both exit and the lights dim. A long silence. Narissa, the plant, moves slightly.

Scene 2

At Rise, the next morning. The lights turn on as Leon enters, followed by Ashley.   Narissa, the plant, is missing from its usual spot.

LEON
...Now, I wasn't able to find someone else willing to donate blood; everyone I asked turned me down, and some gave me really strange looks, even when I told them my cause. But that's okay, I think I might be able to --

ASHLEY
Leon?

LEON
Yes? What is it?

ASHLEY
...Where's Narissa?

LEON
Ashley, have I ever told you about my dream?

ASHLEY
(Under her breath) Yes, many times...

LEON
I aspire to find a way to allow humans to adopt the ability to photosynthesize. Imagine it! Children in poverty stricken countries will no longer have to starve so long as the sun is out. And I will become known across the globe as the botanist who saved countless lives!

ASHLEY
Yeah... but that still doesn't explain why you had to take MY blood.

LEON
You see, my dear Ashley, I need a sample of human blood in order for the serum to be more compatible with the human body. A small price to pay for solving world problems. . Plus... I'm afraid of needles.

>   *He frowns.*

Hm... no reaction... I think I'm going to need another sample.

>   *He moves towards ASHLEY, another syringe in hand.*

ASHLEY
OH no, not this time!

>   *She dodges him.*

They both struggle and end up knocking the vial with the serum onto a large plant with large, brightly colored thorns.

>   *They freeze and look at it in horror.*

Oh god... Leon, I'm so sorry.

LEON
My serum... you spilled it.

He seems to be in shock for a moment, then suddenly goes and retrieves another vial.

LEON *(cont.)*
Good thing I've got a lot more of it to test on! Had you going for a second there, didn't I?

ASHLEY
Hey! That really scared me! I actually thought I had ruined your project...

Don't call me that.

LILLY
Excuse me. Raelyn, yeah. She's not very talkative.

A silence takes the room for a few moments

SETH
… Wh-Why're you here?

LILLY
Huh? Oh. *(clears her throat, puffs out her chest, and tilts her head up slightly. Her next words are to sound rehearsed)* Alcohol and heroin dependency, cutting, and boundary issues. *(smiling)* But, I don't like to just talk about that. I mean, that's not who we are, that's just… other stuff, y'know. Let's talk like we just met at a… train station! Have you ever been on a train?

SETH
Uhm… No, I've seen them… But I don't really travel much… Just long car rides, really…

LILLY
Well, trains are really nice, you should ride on one someday.

SETH cracks a small smile

SETH
I… wasn't really expecting this.

LILLY
What?

SETH
… When they told me I was being sent to a… mental health hospital, I imagined---

LILLY
An asylum?

SETH
N-no… Well… Yeah… *(chuckles nervously)*

LILLY
Pssssht, yeah, most people do. It's actually pretty nice in here, though, and when they bring those big maple donuts for breakfast…

LILLY makes a loud mmm sound, which causes RAELYN to squint over for a moment. SETH giggles lightly. LILLY follows suit, giggling until she speaks again.

LILLY (cont'd)
Yep, living the good life. Just avoid Ms. Davis, she's a bit cranky, like, always.

RAELYN
This isn't summer camp.

The room is silent for a few moments.

LILLY
Right. Sorry. Just trying to make light out of a---

RAELYN
When are you leaving?

LILLY
… I don't know. I---

RAELYN
Why don't you? I'm counting the minutes until my legal hold's over. I'm sick of this place. Sick of the staff. Sick of people without real---

LILLY
Excuse me?!

RAELYN
What?

LILLY
I have real issues, don't you---

RAELYN
Oh, really? Really? I find that hard to believe. You're not recovering from your stupid addictions. You're being stupidly happy. Aren't you supposed to be in a rehab center? Not a hospital for---

LILLY
I almost died of a heroin overdose the day before I was brought here. My mom doesn't believe in… treatment, or whatever, so the only way the doctors could get me in here was a legal hold. My mom still won't budge, so no matter how hard my psychiatrist here tries to find a rehab center, my mom won't offer her permission. I'm here so I don't… Just, shut up, okay? I deal with things my own way. I'm… trying to not let the withdrawals get to me. I feel dizzy all the time because of the meds…

The whole room is silent for a few moments

RAELYN
I'm… sorry. I didn't…

LILLY
It's fine. I'm just… gonna go to my room. See ya, Seth.

SETH gives a small wave as LILLY leaves the room. RAELYN lets her gaze drop back to the radio. Silence takes the room
SETH and RAELYN sit alone in the room now. SETH awkwardly sits on the far end of the

couch. RAELYN remains in the same place, by the radio.

SETH
… Is that… on?

RAELYN shakes her head, but continues to stare directly at the radio.

SETH
Why're you… looking at it, like that, then?

RAELYN
It's the only digital clock in here with seconds displayed.

SETH
… So what's---

RAELYN
I'm not going to rip your vocal chords out if you speak too quickly. They're searching my room. I'm waiting until I can back in.

SETH
S-Sorry… I just---nevermind---Why?

RAELYN
You're asking too many questions. This place isn't for conversation. It's for---should be for---recovery.

SETH
Then what do I… say?

RAELYN
You spew about your problems. They give you medication. Make sure you aren't too suicidal anymore. Then they release you.

SETH
M-medication?

RAELYN
Yeah. Lexepro, Prozac, Trazodone, Zoloft. That kind of medication.

SETH
… I don't think… medication will really… help.

RAELYN
(sarcastic) It's pumping you full of chemicals to reduce your emotions. How could it not help?

SETH
I just… They told me I have a… clinical… issue, and I need…

RAELYN stares at him with a blank expression.

SETH
Sorry, yeah, I…

RAELYN
Be more confident with your words.

SETH
I don't, uh, want… to---

RAELYN
Say that sentence without pauses or uh's. Try again.

SETH
I don't want to, uh---

RAELYN
Again.

SETH
I don't want to, like---

RAELYN
That counts as a pause.

SETH
I don't want to make you mad or anything!

RAELYN
You'd be significantly less annoying if you weren't afraid of offending me. Try telling me why you're here. With as little pauses as possible.

SETH
I'm here because, uhm---

RAELYN
Nope.

SETH
I'm here because I tried to hang myself.

RAELYN
Why?

SETH
I'm sad for no reason. Really, no reason. I have a good family, a bunch of good friends, but I'm just sad, and I take everything personally, and it's stupid, and… I'm sorry, I don't make much sense, I'm sorta… bad with words, it--- Shit. Sorry, sorry… I know I'm not supposed to do that self-degrading thing. It sorta just comes naturally, I guess? I don't know if… I'm trying to be a good person and not a narcissist or

something or if I actually hate myself. Hell... A lot of things I do are to appear nice. I don't think, uh, I know who I am anymore. I'm just that quiet kid who holds the door open for strangers, but can't work up the courage to look them in the eye and smile, huh? I try so hard, y'know, but it's like, not enough, I guess.

RAELYN
Nice tangent.

SETH
... Shut up.

    RAELYN smiles a bit at that.

Scene 2

    A day has passed. RAELYN is in the same place, while SETH is now sitting at the table.
    LILLY has returned, and is laying on the couch, staring at the ceiling. SETH and LILLY
    are eating, but RAELYN doesn't have a plate.

SETH
So... Did they finish searching your room, or whatever?

RAELYN
They did. But they're at it again today.

LILLY
Why's that?

    RAELYN doesn't answer. The room is silent for a moment. LILLY beckons SETH over.
    SETH stands, then goes to sit on the couch.

LILLY
You're a lucky bastard, they served maple donuts today.

SETH
What? I must've... missed it.

LILLY
Really? Have mine, here.

    LILLY hands over the donut. SETH hesitates before taking it.

SETH
Are you sure?

LILLY

Yeah!

SETH takes the donut, and begins to nibble on it.

SETH
You're so nice, Lilly.

LILLY shrugs

Scene 3

*RAELYN is still at the table, as she has been from the beginning. SETH is now across from
her, and they play chess. LILLY walks in after a short while.*

LILLY
Hey guys, the food cart was running behind schedule, so Mr. Ryan had me go down to the preteens' place.
Gotcha guys some spaghetti!

*SETH gives a wave, RAELYN does not look up from the board. LILLY places two
plates next to RAELYN and SETH, then sits on the couch to eat her own meal. SETH
immediately begins to eat, though slowly. However, RAELYN doesn't touch her food.*

SETH
You gonna eat that?

RAELYN
No.

SETH
Can I…?

RAELYN
Sure.

SETH begins to take RAELYN's plate, but LILLY stands.

LILLY
Wait, Seth, don't.

SETH
Huh?

LILLY
Rae Rae---

RAELYN
Don't call me that.

LILLY

Sorry, Raelyn. The entire time you've been here, the only things you've eaten were granola bars Mr. Ryan made you eat. What's up with that?

RAELYN
This place... ruins my appetite.

LILLY leans on table.

LILLY
Raelyn, you gotta eat something.

RAELYN
The human body can survive up to---

LILLY
Sure, yeah, but it's not healthy.

RAELYN
Neither are dirty needles and shots.

LILLY is obviously agitated by this, but takes a breath, and continues.

LILLY
I've seen anorexics before, Raelyn.

RAELYN
And what do you know about it? All you do is binge and overdose. I don't see how you'd know anything---

SETH
(quietly) Guys, please don't fight...

LILLY
Don't you bring my fucking story into this! I'm trying to help you, you, you---

SETH
(slightly louder) Guys...

RAELYN
I don't care what you're trying to do. You don't have any right to---

SETH
(getting louder) Guys...

LILLY
I have full rights to say whatever the hell I want! I can say anorexia is stupid, and you're not doing anything but making yourself look like a fucking skeleton!

SETH
(louder) Guys.

RAELYN
No you don't! No you fu--

SETH
(shouting) GUYS!

RAELYN and LILLY look over to SETH.

SETH
Quit fighting! Just… Quit it. This isn't the place… We're all… dealing with things, let's just… help each other. Please.

LILLY nods, and RAELYN sighs.

RAELYN
… Yes, I… have an issue with eating. It was supposed to be a short thing. To get my step-dad to stop calling me fat. And to… make me feel better about myself. But… I just got used to it. I don't have any appetite. I just… don't move much and I'm fine. My real dad made me come here. It was… getting hard to walk. I'm going to be sent to a rehabilitation center, after tomorrow.

SETH
… Raelyn, you don't---

RAELYN
Please don't say I'm beautiful. Please. It's worthless, really. I hear it all the time. "You're not fat! You're so beautiful. You don't need to do that!" It's sickening to hear the word beautiful.

LILLY
(sighs) Raelyn… I sorta figured out I can't dwell in one place, I need to keep moving. Recovery's like, walking against hurricane winds, no matter what you're fighting. I'm not strong enough to go very far on my own, but that's why I'm here. The staff of this place has a big-ass truck, and they sorta throw kids with issues inside. Then, they have a personal trainer training us to walk with less help, and eventually we'll reach that point where we won't have to fight the winds anymore, the safe place we're going to doesn't have the winds. We'll be able to live life and see everything wonderful and beautiful and not be stuck drinking to escape or cutting to feel like we exist, we'll be… fine. And really fine, not like the fine you say when your parents are all concerned and you want them to go away. No, really fine. And I don't know about you guys, but being fine will be enough to make me real happy. I guess that's why I want to recover. But… to recover, you need to be the first to hold your ground against the winds, or fight them. Otherwise, you'll be blowing away too fast for the truck to catch you.

A long silence takes the room after LILLY's speech. After a few still moments, RAELYN
slowly stands up, struggling to move from her spot, and stumbles slightly. SETH goes to
support her, and LILLY follows suit. RAELYN first picks up the plate she pushed away, then heads for the couch, and sits there. She takes a deep breath, and takes a small nibble of the food. She looks sickened by the aroma, but she forces herself to chew down a small bite.

LILLY (cont'd)
Thank you.

LILLY (cont'd)

… I'm going to court today, after the evening group.

SETH
… Court?

LILLY
CPS decided it'd be best to try and emancipate me from my mom. So I wouldn't need her permission to go to rehab. I'm probably not coming back after that.

SETH
(unsure what to say) … I hope… it goes… well?

> *RAELYN stands again, and slowly moves to*
> *hug LILLY. LILLY, surprised by this action, slowly returns it.*

RAELYN
Thank you.

Scene 4

> *RAELYN is laying on the couch, staring at the ceiling, alone in the room. Soon enough,*
> *SETH bounds in, which causes RAELYN to smile slightly.*

SETH
Ms. Davis said we can go out on the patio!

RAELYN
And Lilly said she was mean. *(chuckles)*

SETH
C'mon!

RAELYN
(gives a hostile, blank stare) You're forgetting I can barely move on my own.

SETH
Oh, right… Uh… Sorry…

RAELYN
(holds the expression for a few moments, then smiles and stands) No, I'm kidding. *(beat)* I meant the stare. I was kidding about the stare. Not the moving thing.

SETH
Oh! Right.

> *SETH hurries to RAELYN, supporting her as they walk offstage. SETH comes back*
> *onstage after a few moments.*

SETH

I don't remember my stay as clearly as I'd like to. Sessions crammed and blurred together, but tiny fragments of the time between sessions remain. Hearing myself laugh. Lilly saying something crazy. Waking up each morning to see the bags under my eyes fading. Rae Rae watching me with those eyes of hers as I moved my bishop up the board. Slowly realizing what Lilly meant by feeling really fine.

Rae Rae left a day before me. She got placed in a rehab she chose. Somehow she managed to send me pictures, she must've smuggled a phone in, or something. This one time, she sent me a picture of a girl that looked almost like a skeleton, saying "Am I this fat? LOL!" Luckily she gave up with text language as fast as she got into it.

One day, she sent me a picture of this girl I didn't even recognize. It was her, making some silly face. Somehow, the beauty in her eyes seemed to have went and filled in the parts of her that were sucked to the bone. She'd gained weight, and she was stunning.

Lilly… You landed a job as a secretary. It apparently didn't pay much, but I could tell how happy you were with it. You called me the day you burned your mom's contact info. You bought a small townhouse with your new fiancé, and built a little treehouse, where you somehow grew flowers. You'd try to get alone time up there, but I don't think it really worked out too well, considering how many texts I got from you. You weren't the type to be alone. You made tons of new friends at work, including your fiancé.

A few nights before your wedding, an old friend visited you. The last text I got from you was "He got me a dime bag. Don't worry, it's just one hit, and this stuff is less than what I used to take." *(he shuts his eyes, and takes a breath, holding back tears)* The next morning, your fiancé gave me the news.

He let me have the first thing you bought when you separated from your mom; a necklace with a flower made of turquoise. Every year, on the date when you gave us the wind speech, Rae and I visit your old treehouse, and we put another potted flower in there. Then, we stand on a tall building's roof, or go on a ferry ride, and let the wind blow across our faces.

We're happy now, and it's because of you, Lilly. So thank you, again.

SETH kneels, and lays the flowers down. RAELYN enters, and goes to lock arms with SETH, giving him a quick peck on the cheek.

RAELYN
C'mon, babe. Let's go.

SETH nods, and SETH and RAELYN walk offstage.

END OF PLAY

Together, Selfless
By Sydney Luke-Hamasaki

Characters:
Reed: 19, female just starting out in college, University of Colorado Boulder, as a psychology major. All their life, they were very grounded and did well in school. Their family was middle class, but Reed's father left when they were young. Reed has an older brother that they will sometimes speak to, but never to their mother. Reed is very emotionally vulnerable.

Blade: 25, a fifth year senior in college and wants to be a mortician when he finally graduates. Suave, dark, mysterious, manipulative, serious and looks very dangerous. Secretly self conscious, volatile and angered easily. Becomes Reed's lover. Uses dry humor, never really trying to be funny.

Ana-Mia: 24, very sweet and trustworthy, but inside she is hurt and angry. She can convince people she is trying to help them while actually make them feel worse. Looks thin and very pale, but she is mostly seen is long, oversized clothes. She desperately want to feel pretty.

Setting (s):
Scene 1,2,3,4,5,6,7 & 8: Reed's bedroom. It is a studio apartment, with a twin/queen sized bed, a night table with a lamp, a chest of drawers topped with books, a floor length mirror and an old bathtub. The kind where it sits independent from the floor. There is one door, the front door, and a large window. Other furniture may be added as the director sees fit, as well as adjusted for mentioned holidays.

Scene 1:
At rise, REED is walking into the room carrying her bookbag. REED goes to open the curtains and throws them open, letting in the light. Afterwards dropping the bag on the bed and taking out a journal. REED sits on the bed, setting the journal on her lap.

REED
Monday, psychology from eleven to two thirty. English lit at four. Home by seven. Tuesday, no class. Wednesday, English at nine to noon, then math at two. Home by six. Thursday and Friday. Bio from eleven to one. Lab at three. Home by eight. Saturdays, call my brother. *(a knock on the door)* Um...c-call my *(another knock)* What the heck? Who is it?

BLADE *(O.S.)*
Is your car parked in front of the main door?

REED
Do I need to move it?

BLADE *(O.S.)*
I'm pretty sure you should move it. You don't want the cops coming around later and picking it up. But that's not why I'm here.

REED goes to the door and looks through the peephole standing on her toes.

REED

Um, well why are you here then? Who are you? Do I actually need to move my car? Guy outside my door?

BLADE
My name is Blade, I live downstairs and I saw you the other day and wanted to welcome you. There is a sticker on your car for CU Boulder. You're a new student there right?

REED
Yeah. So do I need to move my car or not?

BLADE
...Yes.

REED
Fine, whatever. I'll move it now. Hello?

       BLADE has walked away.

REED *(cont.)*
Hello?

       REED opens the door and looks out. REED exits.

                Scene 2:
     Enter REED and BLADE through the front door.

BLADE
I'm sorry I scared you, Reed. I really didn't mean to.

       BLADE shuts the door.

REED
It's fine. It might be good to know some people in the neighborhood. You wanna tell me about yourself?

BLADE
My name is Blade. I'm twenty five. I live downstairs.

REED
(Mocking) Hi, I'm Blade and I'm boring and I live downstairs.

BLADE
Shut up! I'm not boring! I can be *(Eyes REED)* ...real fun if you want me to be. Especially for a pretty girl like you.

REED
Oh really? Why don't you tell me what makes you so fun?

BLADE

Well, fine. I also go to The University of Colorado Boulder, second year senior woop woop, and I want to be a mortician.

> *REED goes to interrupt, but BLADE continues.*

BLADE *(CONT.)*
And before you say anything, no, being around dead people does not scare me, nor does it creep me out. I love the snow, and I hate summer. Both my parents died when I was seventeen in a...car...crash.

REED
I'm sorry Blade. My dad left when I was little. It's not really the same thing, but… anyways. How are you doing now? Do you have a job?

BLADE
Fine, and yes. I'm a secret drug dealer. Don't tell anyone.

REED
Oh good. I could really use a drug dealing friend in this point in my life.

> *Both feel awkward.*

REED *(CONT.)*
I was totally being serious.

> *They laugh.*

REED *(CONT.)*
Okay. I'm done. I'm calm. Why do you wanna be a mortician? And don't say something like "I love dead things." Or dead people…*(Rushed, nervously)* I'd rather you say dead things than dead people, but they are both terrible so just give me something else. Wow am I talking fast? I am aren't I? I start rambling when I get nervous. Not that you make me nervous, I just think you're really hot. Did I just say that out loud? I did...I should stop. Stopping. And don't say you like dead things.

BLADE
(Laughing) So you want me to lie? Kidding, kidding. No, I love watching crime TV and I kind of just got attached to the idea when I was a lot younger. My mom used to tell me I would grow up to be a serial killer or something. Oh. And I love dead things. Your turn.

REED
I'm Reed, and I'm boring.

> *BLADE looks irritated.*

REED *(CONT.)*
(Laughing) I kid, I kid.

BLADE
Why don't we start with how old you are?

This conversation is said sarcastically. BLADE is slightly frustrated.

REED
I am 47. Well 48 in a few months.

BLADE
Damn you look good for 47.

REED
I try.

BLADE
No but seriously.

REED
I'm seriously 57.

BLADE
Oh so now you're in your fifties?

REED
I can time travel. It's a gift.

BLADE
Well why don't you travel back to now and tell me how old you are?

REED
Nineteen.

BLADE
You don't look nineteen. *(Eyeing REED)*

REED
Don't ruin this Mr. Blade.

BLADE
Not trying to. Continue.

REED
Well I'm studying psychology, my mother's choice. She said I needed a more "practical" degree, but I wanted to be an artist. My dad was an asshole and left when I was little. So it was just me, my mom and my brother.

BLADE
My mom, brother and I.

REED
Me, my mom and my brother. We lived in San Diego my whole life. That place has no weather. I did well in high school, and after graduation I went to stay with my friend Mitch in San Francisco for a year.

BLADE
Was he gay?

REED
What? No! Why.

BLADE
Because gay men live in San Francisco.

REED
Not true, gay men live everywhere.

BLADE
Everywhere meaning San Francisco, with you…

REED
Not sure a gay guy would try and hit on my mom.

BLADE
Is she hot?

REED
Dude!

BLADE
It's an honest question.

REED
No.

BLADE
No, it's not an honest question? Or no, she's not hot.

REED
Fine, yes *and* no.

BLADE
To what question?

REED
You're stupid.

BLADE
You didn't answer my question.

REED
(Annoyed) Honestly Blade!

BLADE
Yes honestly! I can't have you lying to me! Duh.

REED
Fine, ask a real question then.

BLADE
Who was Mitch?

REED
He was my best friend and a kick ass tattoo artist. Actually, he gave me my first tattoo.

BLADE
Was?

REED
Well, he kind of died.

BLADE
Oh shit...I'm sorry about that.

REED
It's fine. It's not like there was anything anyone could do. We went out and he had too much to drink and got on his motorcycle... really stupid on his part though. I mean really. I don't drink and I don't see why anyone would. It's just a way to cover up what's really wrong. That's why people get drunk right?

BLADE
You could have though.

REED
I could have what?

BLADE
Could have saved him. I mean, if you had kept him from drinking that night, he would still be alive now.

REED
No! There was nothing that I could do because you can't change people's decisions!

BLADE
Okay then.

REED
I'm sorry. I didn't mean to make you mad, it's just that... I don't know.

BLADE moves closer to REED. BLADE wraps his arms around REED in attempted comfort.

BLADE
I could make you feel better.

REED
How?

BLADE
Like this.

> *BLADE takes REEDs wrist and kisses it.*

> *Scene 3:*
> *At rise, REED is lying in bed, awake looking at the ceiling with her phone in their hand.*

REED
It's 11:57pm and I am sitting alone in my bed waiting for it to be midnight so that I can call my brother who won't be awake because it's like two o'clock in mother fucking New York. And he had to go and move across the country and be super far away and live in a place with "weather." Colorado has weather.

> *REED gets out of bed and starts pacing the floor.*

REED *(CONT.)*
Colorado has freaking weather, Tyler. Jesus! *(Mockingly)* Hey Reed, I'm moving to New York so calling me will never ever be convenient! Not that I actually really want to talk to you… I mean, I do but...this is stupid. Oh, 12:01am.

> *REED dials a number, it rings. No answer.*

REED *(CONT.)*
Wow asshole! Thanks for answering my phone call. It's Saturday, just like we agreed. You know maybe once in a while you could pick up your phone and talk to me instead of doing whatever it is people do in New York. Maybe next Saturday. Bye.

REED throws the phone across the room and screams. There is a knock at the door.

ANA-MIA *(O.S.)*
Can you shut up, please? What is with all the yelling at one in the morning?

> *REED goes to the door and opens it.*

REED
I'm really sorry. I um…

ANA-MIA
Bad night?

REED
How could you…

ANA-MIA
Oh honey, you are screaming to an empty apartment in the middle of the night. You look terrible and you opened the door to a complete stranger without even asking who it is. Bad night.

ANA-MIA extends her hand.

ANA-MIA
Ana-Mia.

      They shake hands.

REED
Reed.

ANA-MIA
I live downstairs. Blade told me you moved in a little while ago. Mind if I come in?

REED
Blade told you about me?

ANA-MIA
No your damn freakout told me about you, honey. Can I come in?

REED
I guess. But I really should be going to bed. I need to get at least a little sleep before my test tomorrow.

ANA-MIA
Oh don't worry, I won't stay long.

      REED steps aside and lets ANA-MIA inside.

ANA-MIA *(CONT.)*
We could do great things with this.

REED
Excuse me, what?

ANA-MIA
Oh, nothing. *(She walks around and picks up things and puts them down. She stops and looks at herself in the mirror)* What are you studying? I'm a theatre and dance major, top of my senior class. I also do modeling on the side. No big deal.

REED
Oh, I'm studying psychology. I'm a freshman.

ANA-MIA
Oh, I admire that. Young, smart, ambitious. We will do great things together, Reed. I will make sure you do well in college.

REED
Thank...you?

ANA-MIA
So what else is there to know about you?

REED
Well, I'm nineteen. I'm from California and I'm really tired.

ANA-MIA
Who were you fighting with on the phone?

REED
My brother. Wait, we weren't fighting. We are supposed to talk every Saturday so I called him and he didn't answer. Which makes me really, freakin pissed because he is the one who moved across country to New York and now isn't awake to take my calls.

ANA-MIA
He's probably with his super model girlfriend when you call. You know how it is.

REED
No, I don't. He isn't superficial like that. He wouldn't even look at a model like that.

ANA-MIA
But you would.

REED
Wait what?

ANA-MIA
Well, I will let you get some rest now. We should hang out some time.

REED
Um, sure. Hey wait. Before you leave, Ana-Mia, do you have two first names? Or is that your first and last name? Or...

ANA-MIA
I will leave these here for you. They can be really helpful. *(Opens a drawer, puts a small pill box and a small bottle in the drawer and closes it)* See you later Reed.

     ANA-MIA walks off stage.

REED
Yeah. You never answered my question...

ANA-MIA (O.S.)
You look nice.

Scene 4:
At rise, REED enters through the door dragging BLADE by the hand. They sit on the bed, close. Both have been drinking.

BLADE
So tell me again. He did what?

REED
(Laughing) So I walk into class. You know, Vincent's English lit class. Yeah, so I missed the past, like five or six classes. And I walk in and yell "Everybody clap yo hands!" and everyone claps and it was just so good. I practically died. But the professor just, like looks at me like I'm crazy. And I'm not sure what possessed him to do it but he stood up on his desk and started clapping with everyone. He sent me out of the class of course but whatever.

BLADE
I thought you didn't drink.

REED
I thought you were fun.

BLADE
Oh, you have no idea how fun I can be.

REED
What kind of fun are we talking about?

BLADE takes REEDs arm and pushes up their sleeve. BLADE starts to kiss up from REEDs wrist to where the shirt sleeve covers.

BLADE
All kinds of fun. Especially if you take that shirt off. I could kiss you and we could have so much fun.

        ANA-MIA stands in the doorway.

ANA-MIA
I sure wouldn't take my shirt off if I looked like that.

BLADE
Ana-Mia! What the are you doing here?

ANA-MIA
Just giving some advice to my little friend here.

REED
I took your advice all day. I haven't had anything since yesterday-

ANA-MIA
And look at all the good that did. I mean seriously.

BLADE
(To ANA-MIA) I am taking care of it. *(To REED)* Don't worry about her, I will make you feel so much better. Just take that shirt off for me.

REED
I don't think I really want to.

BLADE
Do it!

ANA-MIA
Tomorrow, again!

ANA-MIA exits. REED takes off the long sleeve, wearing a tank top underneath.

BLADE
Good. *(Kisses up REEDs arm and onto their shoulder)* Isn't this better?

No answer. BLADE pulls on REEDs arm. REED looks hurt.

BLADE *(CONT.)*
Isn't it better?

REED
Yes. Would you like to stay tonight?

BLADE
I would. *(Kisses REED)* Happy birthday.

Scene 5:
At rise, REED and ANA-MIA sit on REEDs bed. They are playing solitaire.

ANA-MIA
So did you go out for Halloween yesterday?

REED
Hell no. I hate Halloween. I just stayed here and got really drunk and listened to loud music. Did you go out?

ANA-MIA
Kind of. I mean, I dressed up, and of course I looked disgusting. Someone invited me to a party but I didn't really want to go and not look nice.

REED
I wish I got invited to parties.

ANA-MIA
Don't, they suck. Anyways, how are you doing with the anniversary and stuff. Blade told me about your friend, from San Fran…Mitch, right?

REED
Yeah…I'm fine. *(Laughing a little)* He would be so disappointed in me if he was here.

ANA-MIA
Well, I'm not disappointed in you. I mean, you made two friends in your building. Two friends who are going to take care of you. And you got into college and moved far away from your family who obviously doesn't love you enough to call or anything. But who needs them? You have us.

       BLADE stands in the doorway.

BLADE
Yes you do.

REED
Blade! *(Runs up to BLADE and kisses him)* I missed you.

BLADE
And I missed you.

REED
Now we can all hang out together.

       The three sit on the bed. BLADE kisses REEDs cheek.

BLADE
We sure can. So what's going on you guys?

ANA-MIA
Well we were just playing solitaire. Wanna play?

BLADE
Cards are boring. We should do something more fun.

REED
What did you have in mind?

ANA-MIA
Okay Blade, you're an asshole.

BLADE
What? I am not! I feel so offended.

ANA-MIA
Yes you are. And so are you Reed.

BLADE
Wow. That's enough.

REED
Guys, can we not fight about this right now?

ANA-MIA

Sure. I'm done here anyways.

ANA-MIA stands and walks to the door.

ANA-MIA *(CONT.)*
I will see you tomorrow morning Reed.

ANA-MIA exits.

REED
I'm really tired Blade.

BLADE
But I just got here.

REED
I don't want to tonight.

BLADE
You don't get to do this to me. *(Stands and back away from the bed)* You don't get to put me on a shelf and leave me there! You don't get to one day just forget about me like I never happened. I matter!

REED
I know you do. *(Stands)*

BLADE
You can't just throw me away!

REED
I'm not! I'm not throwing you away! I can't! I need you.

BLADE
Good.

BLADE walks back and aggressively pushes REED back onto the bed.

BLADE *(CONT.)*
Happy Halloween Reed.

Scene 6:
At rise, REED is coming through the door followed by BLADE. Both are dressed for snow or cold weather.

BLADE
I really don't understand why you wanted to stay here for Christmas. I mean I know I'm great, but still.

REED shoves BLADE.

REED

You are so self absorbed. It's amazing.

BLADE
(Nonchalantly) I'm really not. I just like making up for the self loathing with sarcasm.

> *ANA-MIA in the doorway.*

ANA-MIA
He really does.

> *REED goes to hug ANA-MIA*

REED
Merry... well... merry after Christmas.

ANA-MIA
Merry after Christmas to you too. I brought you a present. It's not much, but I figured that you could really use one.

> *ANA-MIA gives REED a box*

ANA-MIA *(CONT.)*
It's a scale.

BLADE
That's a bit rude Ana, don't you think?

REED
No, it's great actually. I do need to keep track, I mean look at me.

ANA-MIA
Blade, I'd appreciate it if you used my whole name. And it's not rude if it's a gift. I am very giving after all. So, how are we going to celebrate?

REED
There is nothing to celebrate. Christmas is over.

ANA-MIA
There is always something to celebrate, hun.

BLADE
Exactly. We can celebrate just being here. Reed, you found two good friends and that is always something to celebrate. Right?

REED
Of course. I love you guys and I am so glad you are here. You both make me so happy. Why don't we play cards?

BLADE

You know I hate cards. It's so boring. Can we do something fun?

ANA-MIA
Blade, your idea of fun is sex and hurting people and I don't want to be included in that. Thank you very much.

BLADE
No, I like other things.

ANA-MIA
Like?

BLADE
...Fine, we can play cards. But can we at least play poker or something more fun than solitaire?

REED
Poker sounds like fun.

ANA-MIA
Poker. Fine. Whatever.

BLADE
Someone's angry.

The three begin setting up a game of poker.

ANA-MIA
I am perpetually angry Blade.

BLADE
And I am perpetually gorgeous.

REED
Oh that reminds me. *(To ANA-MIA)* How's the modeling thing going?

ANA-MIA
Slow. The last place I went to told me I needed to lose about fifteen pounds to even be considered.

REED
You weigh like a hundred pounds!

ANA-MIA
Yeah. And?

REED
Okay then.

ANA-MIA
I bet eight pounds.

BLADE
Are we British now?

ANA-MIA
More or less.

REED
Ellow govnah' I would quite enjoy some tea love.

ANA-MIA
Where's the queen? Where's the freaking queen?!

BLADE
Why does no one take poker seriously?!

       REED pokes ANA-MIA

REED
I take it seriously. I poke-her seriously.

BLADE
You know what I mean.

ANA-MIA
I don't. Can you explain it to me please, Blade?

BLADE
Ok, fine. You are both idiots.

REED
God Blade, why do you have to be so mean to us?

BLADE
I'm not, I'm just honest.

ANA-MIA
Well, honestly, you are ruining our fun.

BLADE
No, I'm making this fun. See *(BLADE kisses REED)* See? Fun. *(BLADE kisses REED again)*

ANA-MIA
I'm so done. You guys have fun.

      ANA-MIA stands and throws her cards at the two and goes to walk off stage.

ANA-MIA *(CONT.)*
I'll see you tomorrow.

ANA-MIA exists.

REED
Can you teach me how to play poker better?

BLADE
It's all about counting cards. Come here, I can show you.

REED goes to sit on BLADEs lap.

BLADE *(CONT.)*
Watch. *(BLADE starts laying down cards)* One, two, three…

Scene 6:
At rise, REED is laying in the bathtub, legs resting on one side, out of the tub. It is Valentines Day.

REED
I hate Valentines day. Who came up with it anyways? Couples use it as an excuse for everything. *(Mockingly)* Oh, I was a terrible boyfriend this year, better go buy her some chocolates. Oh I am such a perfect girlfriend, he better get me flowers and buy me jewelry and whatever else I want. Oh, its February 14th, I am so getting laid tonight. God people are so annoying. Can't people just be good to each other all the time? Is that so hard? Maybe on a Tuesday, just tell your significant other that you love them. Why don't people care about people like they used to?!

BLADE walks in through the door and kneels by the bathtub.

BLADE
So presents aren't okay?

REED
Blade! I didn't know you were there! Don't look at me!

BLADE
But I love looking at you. Especially like this. *(BLADE reaches and takes REEDs arm and kisses it)* You never take baths.

REED
I know, I hate them. But I don't really want to stand.

BLADE
Why not?

REED
I'm too tired I guess.

BLADE
On this day in history, in 1872, the first bird refuge was authorized.

REED
What?

BLADE
In 1872, the first bird refuge was authorized.

REED
You dork.

BLADE
You have beautiful legs. *(BLADE kisses REEDs calf)*

REED
And you have a beautiful face.

BLADE
So do you.

REED
It's Valentine's day.

> *Long pause. BLADE takes REEDs hand again.*

BLADE
I love you.

REED
And I love you.

BLADE
Do you know what I love most?

REED
What?

BLADE
I love that I can do this.

> *BLADE holds REED's chin.*

BLADE *(CONT.)*
Happy Valentine's day, Reed.

Scene 7:
At rise, BLADE is sitting on the bed with a pile of mail. REED is sitting on the floor bouncing a small ball looking blankly out into the audience.

BLADE
Bill. Bill. Bill...

REED
Toss them.

BLADE
But you have to pay for these. You can't ignore the fact that you have responsibilities.

REED
Bills don't matter if you have nothing to pay for. The government doesn't own me! I don't owe them anything!

BLADE
Well then...here's a letter from your brother.

REED
(Abruptly, like they didn't mean to say this) Damn my brother! Sorry, what? Oh yeah, read it.

    BLADE opens the letter and reads off the paper. BLADE clears his throat.

BLADE
Hey there Reed. I have a couple of things to say but I will start with the usual greeting BS. How are you doing? How is school? What is the weather like? I'm doing well. New York is so different from home. Winter sucked pretty bad. Nearly lost a toe because of the cold. My job is going great. I got a raise a couple weeks ago. Also got a tattoo. It's the kanji Japanese symbol for protector. Got it on your birthday. Happy birthday by the way. Twenty is a big number. Not as great as legal drinking and gambling age, but still great. Now that all the fluff is out of the way, I have a couple things to say.
Firstly, where the hell have you been?! I still call you on Saturdays, but I never get a call back. No texts, no letters, nothing. You broke your promise to me that you would keep in contact after we both moved out.
Second. I proposed to my girlfriend, Misty. We are going to have a winter wedding this December and I want you to come out for it. I will help pay for your plane ticket if you need me to. I really want you and mom to be there. This is important to me.
Thirdly and lastly. I am flying out late July to visit mom and spend some time in the west coast sun for the summer. I want you to come down and the three of us can spend some real family time together. I miss you and I know mom does too. She calls me crying because you don't talk to her anymore. You are making us kind of worried. Please let me know you are okay.
You and mom are the only family I have. Please don't push us away. I love you. Tyler.

So is this Misty girl the model or whatever you and Ana are always hating on?

REED
Yeah. She's like a supermodel or something. And she's tall, and blonde and I hate her.

BLADE
You've never met her…

    BLADE goes to it next to REED and also stares into the audience.

REED
And? She's stereotypical and my brother deserves a real person. Not hooker in a hoe ass skirt and heels. He deserves someone who's normal and boring.

BLADE
Hi, I'm Blade. I'm boring and I live downstairs.

REED
Hi, I'm Misty and I'm a model and I live in really uncomfortable shoes.

BLADE
Hi, I'm Reed. I'm bored and would love something to drink. Glad you asked Reed, because I would love to have a drink right now. Did you ever finish that bottle from the other night?

REED
No. There are two glasses in my night table.

     BLADE goes and gets the bottle and cups. He pours some into the two cups.

REED *(CONT.)*
What do you want to do with your life? I mean not like get a job, have a family, die. I mean like, what do you dream of doing?

     BLADE gives REED a glass and sits down in the same spot again.

BLADE
I would much rather just stay here with you and not think about the future. I want to be happy now. I only know what I want right now. And maybe what I want now will be the last thing I ever want, but at least I would be happy right now. We can't experience the future, we only can experience the now. You know what I mean?

REED
Nope.

BLADE
Drink that and maybe you will get it.

     ANA-MIA walks into the room and joins the two on the floor.

ANA-MIA
She is gonna need more than that Blade.

     ANA-MIA takes out a little pill box and offers it to REED.

REED
How many am I supposed to take?

ANA-MIA
The box says two. But I usually take five or six. You can take as many as you want though.

REED takes six from the box and takes them.

ANA-MIA *(CONT.)*
Can I get some of that Blade?

REED tries to give ANA-MIA the glass, but she declines it. BLADE stands to pour ANA-MIA a glass.

ANA-MIA *(CONT.)*
You need it more than I do. *(BLADE hands ANA-MIA a glass)* Thanks, Blade.

    All three stare into the audience.

BLADE
(To REED) Do you understand yet?

REED
No.

    BLADE takes REEDs arm and starts to kiss from wrist to shoulder.

BLADE
How about now?

REED
I think I'm starting to.

    ANA-MIA takes the pill box and glass from REED.

ANA-MIA
(To REED) How do you feel?
REED
I feel...better.

ANA-MIA
Good. Blade?

BLADE
I got it.

    BLADE picks up REED and lays them on the bed. REED is unconcious now.

ANA-MIA
Looks like I'm done here.

BLADE
You can go.

ANA-MIA

Bye Blade. Bye Reed.

BLADE
See you next time Ana-Mia. Good night Reed.

Scene 8:
At rise, REED stands at center stage. BLADE and ANA-MIA are sitting at REEDs feet.

REED
September 2nd: It was one of my first days at school. I had unpacked all of my boxes and it had been a pretty good day. But then I found a picture of me and Mitch and just completely I lost it. I didn't think I would do it.

REED *(CONT.)*	BLADE
I know that it was a bad decision to start hurting myself, but I deserved it. If I had kept him from drinking, he would still be here.	I know that it was a bad decision to start hurting myself, but I deserved it. If I had kept him from drinking, he would still be here.

REED *(CONT.)*
September 22nd: I haven't talked to my brother in a few weeks. I really miss him. But he sent me a picture of him and his girlfriend. He said he misses me.

REED *(CONT.)*	ANA-MIA
She is a model.	She is a model.

REED *(CONT.)*
I didn't think he would be that shallow, but I guess he changed when he left.

September 29th: Today is my twentieth birthday and I have no one to spend it with except for this bottle of Grey Goose. Most of it's gone now. I guess not drinking isn't really important to me anymore. I skipped class again today and just slept. It's really cold.

REED *(CONT.)*	BLADE
October 9th. I went to class today and my professor asked me about the cuts on my arm.	October 9th. I went to class today and my professor asked me about the cuts on my arm.

REED *(CONT.)*
I didn't stay to give him an answer.

October 30th. Tomorrow will be one year since Mitch died. Can't imagine what he would say to me. I'm sure he would be disappointed.

REED *(CONT.)*
November 2nd. I haven't eaten in two days. I'm really proud of myself.

ANA-MIA
November 2nd. I haven't eaten in two days. I'm really proud of myself.

REED *(CONT.)*
December 19th. It's been a long time since I have written anything in this book. I am supposed to go home for Christmas tomorrow, but I don't think I will be going.

REED *(CONT.)*
December 26th. I got a scale today, figured I could keep track of my weight. My Christmas gift to myself. It said one hundred pounds today.

ANA-MIA
December 26th. I got a scale today, figured I could keep track of my weight. My Christmas gift to myself. It said one hundred pounds today.

REED *(CONT.)*
I have more scars than I can count...but I can try.

BLADE
I have more scars than I can count...but I can try.

REED *(CONT.)*
January 18th. I haven't slept for a couple days.

ANA-MIA
I'm down to ninety two pounds.

REED
February 14th. I hate Valentines day. I hate myself.

BLADE
1872 scars.

ANA-MIA
And eighty seven pounds.

REED
Blood looks really pretty in bath water.

April 23rd. My mom called today. She asked where I have been and why I don't call. I didn't call her back.

May 13th. I got a letter from my brother telling me he's getting married. Said he wants me there. He asked why I stopped calling. Says he misses me and is flying out in July to visit my mom and wants me to come out and we can be a family again. I'm not sure if I will make it to summer.

June 28th. The school year ends in a couple weeks. I stopped going to class months ago.

REED *(CONT.)*
Too many teachers were asking about my
weight.

ANA-MIA
Too many teachers were asking about my
weight.

REED *(CONT.)*
And why I looked so terrible.

REED *(CONT.)*
And how I could wear long sleeves and jeans
in ninety degree weather.

BLADE
And how I could wear long sleeves and jeans
in ninety degree weather.

REED *(CONT.)*
So I just stopped going.

July 1st.

REED *(CONT.)*
2562 scars.

BLADE
2562 scars.

REED *(CONT.)*
And 85 pounds. I am finally considered
underweight. BMI of 14.1

ANA-MIA
And 85 pounds. I am finally considered
underweight. BMI of 14.1

REED *(CONT.)*
Today is July 21st. My brother and my mom are coming up today. They keep leaving messages
for me saying they are worried and no one has heard from me.

ANA-MIA
But after today no one ever will.

BLADE
But after today no one ever will.

REED goes to bring a stool from off stage, sets it center stage.
REED
(Reading from the paper) The world is so delicate. and I don't want to stay in it anymore. To
my mother, you were my mom and my dad and I love you. To my brother, I will see you get
married. Be happy, both of you. Please understand. This is not your fault.

ALL
I did this to myself.

     REED drops the piece of paper onto the floor. REED stands on the stool.
BLADE
I'm sorry.

ANA-MIA
I love you.

REED
Goodbye.

END OF PLAY

Sydney Luke- Hamasaki, playwright (center) with Devon Hollingsworth (right),
Elliot Beltran (right, back), and Vicky Tran (left).

Famekilling
by Jordan Palen

Characters:
Harvey Harvey: 33, Male. A former child star who continued his career into adulthood before dropping off and winding up on hard times. Isn't afraid to speak his mind, sometimes comes off as abrasive.
Jason Lane: 29, Male (of Korean heritage, given surname is Park). Acts friendly and upbeat but has been forced to conceal many secrets because of his life being a famous actor. Tries to put on an agreeable front to be accepted.
Carol Shirley: 42, Female. Jason's manager. Serious and level headed. Doesn't tolerate anything that could be a danger to Jason's career and is very deliberate in her work.

Setting(s):
scene one: Jason's Mansion, Entrance/Living Room
scene two: Jason's Mansion, Jason's Room

Scene One:

At rise, we see the interior of JASON's mansion. A loud knocking can be heard coming from the door on the right.

HARVEY

Hey. Hey, anyone home? ...c'mon. Open up. *(beat)* ...listen, I respect your choice to not unlock your door for me. But I'm gonna try breaking it down anyway if you don't unlock it, alright?!

The door unlocks, CAROL opening it calmly, standing in the middle of the doorframe to block HARVEY's view of the inside.

CAROL

...Mr. Harvey, I'll have you know that breaking and entering is a criminal offense, however minor, and you are in no position to need to convince anyone to be on your side, in or outside of a courtroom.

HARVEY

Look, I wasn't really going to do it anyway. *(trying to look past her)* Where's Jason? Aren't you his manager, shouldn't you have him on a leash or something?

CAROL

I'm not letting you in until you state your business for visiting.

HARVEY

You're not gonna let me in if I say that, believe me.

CAROL

At least you're honest-

JASON

Uh, Miss Shirley? Could you open the door a little more?

CAROL

I'd advise against that, Mr. Lane.

HARVEY

Could you reason with her for me, Jason?

CAROL

(sternly) Jason.

JASON

...Well, I'd gladly let you in, Harvey, but... Why do you want to come in, in the first place? I thought you're retired?

HARVEY

I just want to talk with you, y'know.

CAROL

About what.

JASON

That's supposed to be *my* line...

HARVEY

God, I don't know, can't I just visit someone's house without it being turned into some sorta interrogation deal all of a sudden?! Look, I'm not gonna do anything, I just want some drinks and a little time to catch up on what's been happening, y'know. Let me in.

JASON moves past CAROL, towards the door, but she puts a hand on his wrist. Firm enough to stop him and have him look at her, though she has the control to make it soft, so he doesn't get hurt.

CAROL

Lane, I hope you're careful around him. I don't want you to do anything you'd regret.

JASON

...I will be, Miss Shirley. You don't have to worry.

CAROL takes her hand off from JASON's wrist, allowing him to open the door. HARVEY steps in, and CAROL exits.

HARVEY

Hey, long time no see, huh, Jason? How's life been treating you? *(hovers over a chair)* Hey, s'it okay if I sit here?

JASON

Um. Well, sure. Go ahead, Harvey! ...I've been doing good, yeah. I mean, I've been getting lots of roles and all. I never really knew that I'd get to the point in this career where I'd be more than just a background voice, but... I'm still having trouble believing that I- that I really got to meet you! ...I probably sound like a creep, but I kinda thought of you as an idol way back when. It's sorta like meeting Superman or something, I just... *(he trails off)*

HARVEY

...you just *what.*

JASON

It's been nagging at me a lot, you know... You had everything, and it came so naturally to you, I just don't get why you dropped off all of a sudden. What happened?

HARVEY

God. *(takes a deep sigh as if he's heard the question a million times before)* I thought that you of all people might be able to understand my reasoning for giving up showbiz. You're in it for Christ's sake! I don't get what I can even explain to you that you don't already know!

JASON

...well. I'm sorry, I guess- but I just don't understand why you left. Wasn't it your life? You were performing since you were just a little kid, you were living the dream!

HARVEY

Okay, you have to be kidding me because there is no way that you can think "child actor" and "living the dream" in the same sentence without a sense of sarcasm or horrific naivete.

JASON stares at HARVEY like cattle looking on to an approaching vehicle, staring it in the headlights, too confused to feel as though he's hit a dangerous patch in the conversation.

HARVEY

I was living a manufactured, carefully scheduled and regulated act that the higher ups had the sheer gall to claim was a well adjusted life.

JASON

O-oh.

HARVEY

I really don't know why I had to say that to you. I mean, I've been inside the system my whole life, and you know what? It's shit. It's all just phony processed shit that they force people into so the public can get the same uninventive, boring dredge that they've always been given. And the thing is, once you're stuck in a fake making business, you turn fake yourself. There's people on every angle trying to expose some "terrible secret" you're hiding. I hate that. Everyone's got personal baggage that's nobody else's business, that's how we are. And if there wasn't a reason for secrets then it wouldn't be such a universal goddamn concept. Anyone who's forced a secret out for laughs is just human waste, and the guys who fabricate rumors and make up "forbidden love affairs" are even worse... god, I just couldn't stand it. I had to get out after a while, so I picked up bad scripts, going on the decline of quality until the system and the public deemed me unvaluable. Then I got out free. I tell ya, it's like I'm finally able to be myself now! It's great!

JASON

I can imagine...

HARVEY

Hey. Don't look so down. See, I'm also glad I'm out, because I can talk to you now without the media trying to turn it into some competition. Whoo, I'm parched. Got anything to drink?

JASON

Uh, yeah! I do!

HARVEY

Got anything that can knock my ass to the floor in two minutes?

JASON

W-well, I don't think so... the strongest alcohol I have is wine.

HARVEY

Eh, it's better than nothing. What, are they not letting you get away with getting hammered or something?

JASON moves to pour drinks for HARVEY and himself.

JASON

It's not in my contract, technically, but I prefer to be inhibited rather than not.

HARVEY

You really need to loosen up sometime- wait, I forgot. Contract. Yeah, sorry I brought that up. Probably not a good idea to loosen anything while "the man" has you under his control. *(he laughs and takes a drink from JASON's hand, taking a deep swig)* Jesus, that hits the spot.

JASON

...I'm really sorry that you feel that way about being an actor, Harvey-

HARVEY

Nah, nah, nah, it's in the past now. See, right now I have a drink, someone who's straight with me, and a decently paying job that doesn't take a toll on my mind. I'm done being mad now, let's talk about those things.

JASON

...straight?

HARVEY

I mean, honest, y'know... Even when people pushed for us to be in some sorta competition, you still were frank with me. Shit, for your age, you were downright sportsmanlike. Not a lot of guys take the time to say thanks to the guy they *beat* for being an inspiration to them.

JASON

Oh. Oh, right! ...it's nothing, really, Harvey. I just was speaking my mind, that's... that's nothing special, is it? I mean, everyone does.

HARVEY

Hmm... well yeah, but for you to like, get over the fakeness everyone else was spouting and actually be yourself, that's something admirable. *(takes another drink)* You're really not that bad.

JASON

...I'm, flattered, uh... really. *(pause)* ...I have to go, sorry. *(stands up and starts leaving without saying a word)*

HARVEY

Wait, hey! You left your drink! *(beat)* ...*my* drink now.

HARVEY downs the glass of wine eagerly. CAROL enters stage left as JASON worriedly exits.

CAROL

...did something go wrong, Mr. Harvey.

HARVEY

No, nothing's wrong. I think Jason jus' needed to water his dog 'cause the iron was on or something.

CAROL

Now isn't the time for jokes. I want you to to tell the truth.

HARVEY

Would you believe he ran out on his own and said he needed to go. ...probably taking a leak, actually.

CAROL sighs deeply and sits down on a chair next to HARVEY, she leans her elbow on the armrest, holding her head in her hand.

CAROL

...you didn't say anything that Mr. Lane might have taken offense to, did you.

HARVEY

No, no, I just said he was honest for an actor 'cause the whole acting business was full of crap, none of that's offensive at all.

CAROL

And if I told you that you're surprisingly tactless for someone who wanted to visit someone on good terms, you wouldn't feel even the smallest bit offended?

HARVEY

Hey, hold on here. You're calling me tactless, that's *completely* an insult.

CAROL

I also said that you were visiting on good terms, didn't I? Why would you take offense if I complimented you?

HARVEY

Yeah, but- *(pauses to think)* ...that's still different, I just insulted a business, not Jason.

CAROL

And I'm sure that me directing the insult towards something you care about as opposed to you yourself, then there would be absolutely no justification for you being upset, right?

HARVEY

Is this some sorta manager thing. How the hell are you so good at making me feel like an idiot.

CAROL

Highlighting your ignorance wasn't the point. I want you to apologize to Mr. Lane.

HARVEY

You're saying that like I wasn't going to do it already.

HARVEY begins to sit up, moving to exit to where JASON walked off to. CAROL follows after him.

CAROL

I need to come with you.

HARVEY

Do you have something to apologize for?

CAROL

No, I just believe it would be in your best interest for me to supervise you when you talk to Mr. Lane. I just have the completely justifiable concern that your uncanny ability to nonchalantly swallow your foot in the middle of a conversation will cause more trouble for him. *(pause)* And yourself.

HARVEY

Boy, you *really* don't like to mince words when it comes to me, do you.

CAROL

My mistake, I thought that you preferred honesty in others.

HARVEY

Ow. Jeez, what do you sharpen your tongue on in the morning?!

Both exit.

Scene Two:
CAROL and HARVEY enter JASON's room. JASON is suspiciously not present.

CAROL

Mr. Lane?

HARVEY

I'm sure he went this way- Come on, Jason, open up, will ya?

CAROL

You shouldn't sound too demanding. There's probably a good reason why Mr. Lane is hiding from you.

JASON

(behind a bathroom door) Um, he… hello?

HARVEY

Jason? Hey, look. I came to say I'm sorry for... *(turning to Carol, whispering)* What am I sorry for, again?

CAROL

(whispering) You insulted something that Jason was passionate about.

HARVEY

(talking normally) I'm sorry I said all that stuff about the whole acting business, Jason. I didn't mean anything about it! I'm just talking about... y'know, I don't even hate acting! It's just all the fakeness of the industry that turns me off and all that, desperate clinging for controversy that doesn't exist even. Look, you're probably the most honest person I know and-

JASON

Please! *Stop calling me that!*

HARVEY

...honest?

JASON opens the bathroom door, standing in the door frame and holding his head tiredly.

JASON

Yeah... that. I don't want you to call me that, alright, it's just... *(sighs)* Harvey, I'm sorry I let you down. I admire you. A lot, like... Miss Shirley, I'm- I'm really sorry... I know you probably wanted me to keep this a secret...

CAROL

...Mr. Harvey. You have to be sure to never tell anyone about this. We don't need rumors being spread about Mr. Lane's character...

HARVEY

Well, sure. I'm not gonna leak anything to the press, you two can trust me. What is it?

JASON

...my last name isn't really Lane. It's Park.

CAROL

(flabbergasted) What.

HARVEY

That's it...?

JASON

Yeah, you know, I had to change it when I became an actor. Stage names and all. Plus, Jason Park didn't have the same ring to it that Jason Lane did. It does make for a good joke though like "Wanna take a Park in my Lane?"

HARVEY

Shirley, is he being serious?

CAROL

Well, yes, he's telling the truth- But, Mr. Lane, that couldn't have been the secret you were so nervous about telling Mr. Harvey!

JASON

You sure? Well, actually, yeah, that wasn't what I was afraid of... Sorry, it's... I just wanted to stall for time. Uh. *(takes a deep breath, walks out of doorframe and paces around in his room)* See, the thing is, Harvey- I. I love- I love acting so much, alright? And, I knew about all the things you talked about but, I thought... I just, I know you probably have your own... things, you'd rather have be secret, okay? But... it, I wish it was easier to open up about... how I feel. It's- I, ugh, I'm just scared about being rejected- I want to come out about- I want to come clean, Mr. Harvey! I. You're so, you're really amazing to me! I just want to tell you it, but I'm, working like this, it's like impossible for me to tell you, even in secret I'm just- *(sighs)* I'm sorry.

HARVEY

(beat) ...so, what is it you wanted to tell me?

JASON

For god's sake, *I love you, Mr. Harvey! (pause)* Oh no. I said it, ohhh no, I'm, I'm really sorry... I'll go- leave now...

HARVEY

...this is your house.

JASON

Um, can I go back to the bathroom, then?

HARVEY

Jason- look. I don't mind. Really, I don't. What, were they going to fire you if they found out you had a thing for me?

CAROL

No, that wasn't the issue... as you might recall, however, Jason had to- repress his secrets to be accepted by the public. He isn't exactly confident enough to face the criticism he would have to deal with, if he were ever to be open about his feelings for you.

HARVEY

...yeah, I can imagine...

JASON

I know it's probably too optimistic for me to expect you to return, my feelings, you know... I just- you saying how honest I am, it just made me feel- guilty for hiding it, still.

HARVEY

...still? How long have you, er, thought of me this way?

JASON

Well, I always admired you as an actor... I guess it turned into a crush sometime when I was a teenager, and I wanted to get into acting. You're only four years older than me, and, I just had the stupid idea I might be able to meet you- now that you've dropped out, I've been feeling really awful, but I like acting, and people probably look up to me now, too... But that's a lot of responsibility, sometimes I get too overwhelmed by everything I'm so sorry I'm talking too much...

HARVEY
(puts an arm around Jason's shoulder) Hey, no, don't think that way. Listen, if anyone tries to make you feel like shit over anything, tell me and I'll whip them into shape.

JASON
...y-you'd really do that for me, Mr. Harvey?!

CAROL
Let's hope not, for the sake of his lawyer.

HARVEY
Ha, ha, ha.

JASON
You, really don't know how, relieved I am to hear that, Mr. Harvey... thank you.

HARVEY
Hey, it's no problem. What, do you want to kiss or something?

CAROL
(sternly) Harvey.

HARVEY
I'm not joking this time around, cut me a break!

JASON
...uh, I'll think on that, maybe... do you want to go out with me?

HARVEY
Ha, sure thing. When and where.

JASON
Oh my god, n-no, wait, I meant, going out of my room!

HARVEY
Oh!

ALL
(laughing)

Rúnda
by Gabriela Schnepp

Characters:

Amanda: A teenager visiting her grandfather in Ireland. Originally, she was an upbeat, kind person, but the death of her parents has turned her into a shell of her former self. She is now sad and quiet. She is supposed to be young; not over the age of 18 but older than 12.

O'Connor: Amanda's grandfather. Superstitious and ever so slightly crazy. Old, but wise and sharp with his tongue.

Spiorad: An Irish nature spirit that lives in the wild. The same age range as Amanda. Although feared by O'Connor, he is not actually dangerous is in fact lonely. A little sarcastic, but kind and understanding.

Settings:

Scene 1: A moorish landscape that abruptly cuts off into a steep cliff. Below is the sea. A long distance away from the cliff, a forest of tall trees follows the line of the coast. There is a small hut that is sitting in the middle of the grassy moor. Beside the house is a chicken coop and a small structure for sheep. The sky is dark and cloudy.

Scene 2: Inside the small hut, specifically the kitchen. Plain, with a fireplace in the corner and a small table with four chairs.

Scene 3: Outside the hut, on the porch

Scene 4: A clearing inside the forest. A small patch of light in an otherwise dark area.

Scene 5: Outside the hut, on the porch

Scene 6: A clearing inside the forest. A small patch of light in an otherwise dark area.

Scene 7: Inside the small hut, specifically the kitchen. Plain, with a fireplace in the corner and a small table with four chairs.

Scene 8: A clearing inside the forest. A small patch of light in an otherwise dark area.

Scene 9: Outside the hut, on the porch.

Scene 1:

At rise, O'CONNOR is tending to a small potted plant outside of the hut. He stoops over with age and walks with a slight limp. He whistles to himself as he works.

AMANDA walks onstage, clutching a suitcase. She is not smiling, but instead looks around nervously.

    O'CONNOR glances up.

O'CONNOR
Eh! Maria!

AMANDA
Maria?? Um, sorry... I'm not-

O'CONNOR frowns and hobbles up to her. Scratching his chin, he pulls at her hair. AMANDA yelps.

AMANDA
Hey! Don't do that! Leave me alone!

O'CONNOR

Calm yourself, young one! What're you yelling at anyway? I'm your own flesh and blood, don't you see? Amanda! It's me!

AMANDA
... Grandpa O'Connor?

O'CONNOR
Hee, hee, hee, we both had a scare, now didn't we?

AMANDA
Goodness! I didn't recognize you at all! I guess I've been away longer than I thought!

O'CONNOR
Well, it has been a while, hasn't it? I knew you were coming, but I didn't expect it to be so soon!! Pardon these old eyes... I just haven't seen you 'round since you were... this tall.

>   *He kneels and lifts his hand some way off the ground. AMANDA smiles tenderly.*

AMANDA
I find it hard to believe that I was ever that small, Grandpa O'Connor.

O'CONNOR
It's the truth!

AMANDA
... So... it's nice here... I'll be here for a while, I'm sure you know..... Thanks for letting me stay.

O'CONNOR
(Uncomfortably) I.... why don't you come inside? It's getting cold out here. Besides, you don't want to meet up with Banshee, now do you?

AMANDA
A what?

O'CONNOR
(With a sigh) Looks like we're gonna have to have a little lesson then...

AMANDA
Aren't they pretend, Grandpa? That's what I've heard vaguely.

>   *O'CONNOR grabs her arm gently.*

O'CONNOR
Let's not talk about this. Not right now... you're probably tired, after all.

AMANDA
It has been a long trip... the plane ride was a nightmare...

She chuckles and smiles brightly.

AMANDA *(cont.)*
It wasn't any worse than my FIRST plane ride! I remember that I was SUPER fussy, and poor mom had to-

She breaks off with a small hiccup noise and gently presses her hand against her mouth. The suitcase quivers in her grasp.

O'CONNOR quickly takes the suitcase away and places a hand around AMANDA'S shoulders. It should be hesitant, as if he isn't sure if he's comforting her or making things worse.

O'CONNOR
Come inside, come inside... These winds can be unforgiving. You'll find rest for your weariness indoors.

O'CONNOR *(cont.)*
(To self) Besides... these trees have eyes.

> *(O.S) A wolf howls. AMANDA looks frightened, but O'CONNOR simply guides her offstage.*

O'CONNOR
(Chuckling, but tense) Wolves aren't the things to worry about here.

AMANDA
(Mumbling) Okay Grandpa. Whatever you say...

Scene 2:

At rise, AMANDA is seated alone at the table. There is a picture frame in her hand. She sighs to herself and wipes her nose. O'CONNOR walks in.

AMANDA
(Blandly) Maria. That was my mother's name.

O'CONNOR freezes.

AMANDA *(cont.)*
Maria. You called me Maria when you first saw me. Is there a reason for that?

O'CONNOR
(Softly) Damn these old eyes...

AMANDA
What?

O'CONNOR
My mind isn't what it used to be. I forget. I live in the past.
AMANDA
You thought I was my mother?

O'CONNOR
Yes. You look a lot like she did at your age.

AMANDA puts the picture down and stares out the window

AMANDA
(Softly) I miss them.

O'CONNOR
I know, lassie. I keep glancing down that path, expecting to see your mother's smiling face as she runs to greet me.

AMANDA
I keep expecting to feel a pinch on my cheek whenever I feel sad. Daddy always told me to keep my spirits up.

O'CONNOR
(To himself) Spirits...

AMANDA
I remember coming here as a child. Everything seemed so magical... so unreal...

O'CONNOR
As a child? You're still a child!

AMANDA
I've had to grow up quickly.

O'CONNOR
(Hopefully) But you still find this place magical, don't you? Just like you did when you were just a little thing?

AMANDA
(Bitterly) Why does that matter? It's not like any of that crap I thought of was real.

O'CONNOR opens his mouth to say something, but thinks better of it.
O'CONNOR
I don't think your mother would have liked you to forget to live.

AMANDA
I'm not forgetting. I'm simply thinking another way now. It's funny how life changes when things happen.

O'CONNOR
They loved you, you know that?

There is a pause.

AMANDA
That didn't keep them from dying.

O'CONNOR
Child, if you think that way, nothing is ever going to make you feel happy again.

AMANDA is not angry. She is simply weary

AMANDA
Then I won't be happy. It's the least I can do. My parents were my everything. My everything.

O'CONNOR
Look....

He sits next to AMANDA at the table and takes her hands into his.

O'CONNOR (*Cont.*)
I know that this is a hard time for you. You've lost your parents. I've lost a daughter and a son. Why don't you and I just muddle through this together?

Angry, AMANDA gets up and walks away. O'CONNOR sighs and walks off in the other direction.

Scene 3:
At rise, O'CONNOR is seated on the porch, rocking back and forth. It is morning.
AMANDA enters with a glass of water. She smiles at O'CONNOR and hands him the glass.

O'CONNOR
Ah... thank you, lassie....

AMANDA
You said you wanted to talk to me?

O'CONNOR
(*Confused*) I did?

AMANDA
Yes. Just now, after you asked me to get you a glass of water.

O'CONNOR
.... I... AH YES! Yes I did! Hee, hee, forgetful old mind!

AMANDA
Yes... what is it you wanted?

O'CONNOR
(*Gesturing for her to sit*) Aren't the trees beautiful? And the ocean?

AMANDA
... Yes. I guess they are.

O'CONNOR
The sea and the forest have been here for as long as I can remember. A balance between the two. A perfect harmony.

AMANDA
A harmony.

O'CONNOR
Harmony. Yes, indeed. Harmony between all things living. A magic that is seen through the beauty of nature.

AMANDA
(With a laugh) Every time you say magic, I imagine little leprechauns jumping through the heather.

O'CONNOR
That's absurd!

AMANDA
I know.

O'CONNOR
There's more than just leprechauns in the heather.

AMANDA frowns, shifting to look at her grandfather.

AMANDA
(Slowly) Grandpa... you don't actually believe in magic, do you?

O'CONNOR
Unlike a stubborn young lassie that I know, I choose to let this place of beauty sing its secrets to me. As children grow, they lose that ability to see the wonderful things in front of their eyes. Adults are so... stiff. So practical. They forget to live in their imaginations, and so, the door to magic closes.

AMANDA
Grandpa, are you feeling alright?

O'CONNOR
(With a laugh) What you said was true; you've had to grow quickly. I was hoping that coming back here would make you feel like a child again.

AMANDA
I can't go back to being a child. Not with what happened.

O'CONNOR
Well, I can be child enough for the both of us.

Slight pause.

AMANDA
... What kind of magic?

O'CONNOR
(With a laugh) Couldn't resist the urge, could you?

AMANDA
Do you have any stories?

O'CONNOR
Oh, there's many stories. Many stories, just like there are many creatures.

AMANDA
What about a banshee?

O'CONNOR
Of course, a wonderful place to start!

AMANDA
What is it?

O'CONNOR
Some say that it's the ghost of a woman. A spirit that warns untimely death with her wail.

AMANDA
Why'd you warn me about one anyway?

O'CONNOR
Strange things happen in the woods.

AMANDA
(Scoffs) Are you telling me that there are *banshees* in the woods, Grandpa?

O'CONNOR
Perhaps. At night, anyway.

AMANDA
Grandpa. I don't really liked to be messed with.

O'CONNOR
There's also Selkies in the sea.

AMANDA
(Exasperated) Grandpa!

O'CONNOR
Men and women who take the form of seals... Tell me, is there a more magical place than here?

AMANDA
Grandpa....

O'CONNOR
Elves in the woods.... water horses.... vampires...

AMANDA
Vampires?

O'CONNOR
Oh yes. Vampires. Ghosts and goblins, dark riders....

AMANDA
You're gonna give me nightmares.

O'CONNOR
I'm sorry, lassie. I just thought you should know.

AMANDA
Why are you trying to scare me?

O'CONNOR
I'm not. You have to be prepared in these parts. It isn't the city.

AMANDA
I know. I'll be fine. I won't let any wolves get to me.

O'CONNOR
It's not the wolves you have to worry about.

AMANDA
Grandpa, I'm not a little kid anymore. I know what's real and what's not. You're not fooling anyone.

O'CONNOR
(With a shrug) Suit yourself. Of course, your mother was alway interested in these sort of things.
Another pause.

AMANDA
What was my mother like?

O'CONNOR
(Startled) What?

AMANDA
When she was a little kid, what was she like?

O'CONNOR
Oh, Maria was always full of life. Always asking questions. Always bubbly and curious.

AMANDA
Was she brave?

O'CONNOR
Brave? Well... yes, I guess so. She would wander off on her own after dark, if that's what you mean. She wasn't afraid to dive right into the ocean, or touch spiders or even climb one of those trees. Yes, she was brave. And when she packed up her belongings and went off to places unknown... I dunno. That took bravery as well. Her new life was very different than what she had before. Your father helped her out some, I assume.

AMANDA
Yeah...

O'CONNOR
You had good parents, Amanda. Brave parents. Caring parents. They didn't forget about this creaky old man who sat alone in his hut, wasting away from sadness and loneliness as he watched the sea. They didn't forget. They came back and visited me, at first just as a newly married couple, and then with you.

AMANDA
Was I trouble?

O'CONNOR
(Laughing) Of course! All little children are trouble! That's what makes them children!

AMANDA
...I barely remember...

O'CONNOR
I wouldn't expect you to. But I remember. Yes, you were always running around. Always asking questions.

AMANDA
Just like mom.

O'CONNOR
Just like Maria.

AMANDA
... Grandpa, if I was there with them.. I could have done something.

O'CONNOR
(Exasperated) Done what? It all happens quickly, so I've heard.

AMANDA
But still. I could have... I should have... I should have been there.

O'CONNOR
Lassie-

AMANDA
The last thing I told my mother was that I hated her.

O'CONNOR reels back, shocked.

O'CONNOR
What?

AMANDA
We were in a fight.... I was supposed to go with them, but... I yelled at them, and they left me behind.

O'CONNOR
Amanda-
AMANDA
The last thing I said to my mother was: 'I hate you.'

A long pause.

AMANDA
It's my fault, grandpa.

O'CONNOR
Mothers and daughters fight! That's what happens in a relationship! Nothing is your fault. No matter what, don't think that way. Don't you dare.

AMANDA
How do you do it, grandpa?

O'CONNOR
Pardon?

AMANDA
Stay so positive and wise.

O'CONNOR
Years of pain, believe me. Getting old is no picnic. So take advice from this old man; Don't beat yourself up about the past. You're not doing yourself a favor.

AMANDA
I'm not trying to. I'm giving myself the punishment I deserve since I have no more parents to dish them out.

O'CONNOR
You don't deserve a punishment. Life is already burden enough. Don't carry the guilt of the dead.

AMANDA
But still-

O'CONNOR
I let the magic of this place heal me. Perhaps you should do the same.

AMANDA
I don't believe in banshees.

O'CONNOR
You don't have to. You just have fool yourself.

AMANDA
In that case... *(She stands up)* I'll go explore. Like my mother would.

O'CONNOR
Don't stay long after dark. Come back in before the sunset.

AMANDA
What time is that?

O'CONNOR
(Amused) Do you see a clock around here, lassie?

AMANDA
Good point.

O'CONNOR
Don't wander far.

AMANDA
(With a laugh) Don't worry! I'm brave like mom! I won't let any *banshees* get me.

O'CONNOR
I never said anything about banshees.

    AMANDA kisses his cheek and walks offstage. O'CONNOR takes a long drink from the water glass.

O'CONNOR *(cont.)*
It's the Selkies that I'm more concerned about.

        He stand up and walks offstage, shaking his head sadly.

Scene 4:
At rise, AMANDA is seated in the middle of a clearing in the forest. Her face is in her knees miserably.

AMANDA
Who am I kidding?!? I'm not brave! I can't even walk through the woods without getting lost! I'm a total failure!

Short pause.

AMANDA *(cont.)*
WHY AM I SO USELESS???

She breaks down and begins to sob uncontrollably. This ends up with her curled up on the floor.

Enter SPIORAD. He is hesitant to walk up to AMANDA, taking small steps. His noise is masked by AMANDA'S sobs.

SPIORAD
Are you going to cry all day and kill the ferns with your salty tears?

AMANDA bolts upright, horrified and frightened.

AMANDA
What the hell- WHO ARE YOU??!?

SPIORAD
(Blandly) Honestly, you're scaring the birds away with your wailing. You're worse than a banshee.

AMANDA
Look, I don't know who you are, but I want you to leave me alone!!

SPIORAD
Of course you'd say that. After all, how would you know that these are *my* woods?

AMANDA
(Offended) Your woods? *Excuse* me?

SPIORAD
My woods.

AMANDA
(Sarcastically) I didn't know the woods *belonged* to anyone. *Pardon* my trespassing. I'm sorry that I *intruded.*

SPIORAD
Good, as long as you know your mistake.

AMANDA
(Dryly) I was being sarcastic, you moron.

SPIORAD
(Confused) Sar..... cast-ic?

AMANDA
Sarcastic.

SPIORAD
What's that?

AMANDA

(Surprised) Sarcastic? You don't know what that means?

SPIORAD
(Sheepishly) I don't get around much.

AMANDA
I don't know whether to feel really sorry for you or to laugh.

SPIORAD
Typical human..

AMANDA
Excuse me?

SPIORAD
Of course you'd say that.
AMANDA
(With a sigh) Look, I'm sorry... I'm just a little stressed out right now is all.

SPIORAD
(Gently) That's all right, I guess.

An awkward pause.

AMANDA
Why are these *your* woods anyway?

SPIORAD
Because I've lived here for years.

AMANDA
Seriously? I think my grandpa would have mentioned you.

SPIORAD
Grandpa? You don't mean *O'Connor*, do you?

SPIORAD
Did he mention spirits?

AMANDA
Yes, and a few other things. Silly, huh?

SPIORAD
(Mostly to himself) Then he *did* mention me... Huh... of course he did.

Another awkward pause.

AMANDA
I'm sorry, but who the hell are you?

SPIORAD
(Dryly) You're just *now* asking that?

AMANDA
(Annoyed) I asked before, but you didn't answer.
SPIORAD
(Proudly) I'm called Spiorad.

AMANDA
Spiorad?

SPIORAD
(Confident) Yes.

AMANDA
That's a weird name.

SPIORAD
(Deflated) Oh... Well, what's *your* name then?

AMANDA
Amanda.

SPIORAD
HA!

AMANDA
(Insulted) What's the matter *now*?

SPIORAD
(Smug) That's the *weirdest* name I've ever heard.

AMANDA
Are you just repeating what I've said before to make me feel bad?

SPIORAD
(Lying) No.

AMANDA
Liar.

SPIORAD
Hm! Well at least I'm not crying my eyes out on the floor in the middle of nowhere!

AMANDA
And what are *you* doing in the middle of nowhere?

SPIORAD

I told you! I live here!

AMANDA
And *why* is that?

SPIORAD
A long story.

AMANDA
I have time.

SPIORAD
It's getting dark.

AMANDA
I feel like you're hiding something.

A long pause.

SPIORAD
Look... Anunda?

AMANDA
Amanda.

SPIORAD
Amanda. Would you freak out if I told you I was a Nature Spirit?

AMANDA
Yes.

SPIORAD
I'm a Nature Spirit.

AMANDA
I really don't understand boys.

SPIORAD
(Amused) I didn't expect you to believe me. Of course, your Grandfather isn't exactly *fond* of me.

AMANDA
I'm not following.

SPIORAD
He's afraid of me.

AMANDA
(Dryly) Who wouldn't be? I think you're almost as crazy as him.

SPIORAD
Why do you say that?

AMANDA
Well, you live in the *woods*, apparently... You're telling me that you're a ghost-

SPIORAD
(Offended) I *do* beg your pardon! I never said that I was a *ghost*! Gosh, were you even *listening*?

AMANDA
I *was* listening! You said you were a Nature Spirit!

SPIORAD
(Annoyed) There's a *big* difference, mind you!

AMANDA
Like what, oh knowledgeable master?

SPIORAD
I'm not dead. That's a big one.

AMANDA
(Sarcastically) Oh *sorry*!

SPIORAD
There, you see?

AMANDA
(Exasperated) I'm lost in the woods, and a creepy boy keeps telling me that he's some sort of supernatural being.

SPIORAD
I never said I was supernatural. I'm as natural as the trees here.

AMANDA
(Ignoring him) You sound like my grandpa. He's been telling me *all* about Irish Magic. And now *you're* saying the same things.

SPIORAD
Then maybe it's time you started taking him seriously.

AMANDA
I'm *done* being the wide-eyed little kid. When the rug's pulled out from under your feet, it hurts you more.

SPIORAD
I feel like something's not right with you.

AMANDA

I'm not comfortable talking about this with you. You're a stranger to me, remember?

SPIORAD
I told you my name.

AMANDA
That doesn't matter. I don't know who you are at all.

SPIORAD sits.

SPIORAD
Well, we've got to start SOMEWHERE, right? Why don't you tell me why you've come into the woods in the first place?

AMANDA hesitates. If she is standing. she should sit down next to SPIORAD. If she is still sitting, she should just shrug.

AMANDA
I'm just visiting my grandpa for a bit, while this whole ordeal blows over.

SPIORAD
Yes, I was surprised when I found you wandering. I've kept an eye on O'Connor and I haven't seen you around. Although I do tend to keep a healthy distance. If he sees me, he likes to shoot at me.

AMANDA
(Appalled) But- he wouldn't shoot at a boy in the woods!

SPIORAD
I'm not just a boy. I'm a-

AMANDA
(Exasperated) Right, right... you're a Nature Spirit or ghost or whatever. How long are you gonna keep the act up?

SPIORAD
For as long as it takes for you to start believing me.

AMANDA
I don't believe you.

SPIORAD
I know. Such a shame.

Short pause.

SPIORAD
'While this whole ordeal blows over?'

AMANDA

My parents died.

SPIORAD
(Uncomfortable/Surprised) Oh. Oh, I...

AMANDA
It was a car crash.

Long pause.

AMANDA *(cont.)*
You don't know what a car is, do you?

SPIORAD
(Embarrassed) No.

AMANDA
I can't really tell if you're lying or not... You don't seem like you are.

SPIORAD
I'm not.

AMANDA
Still, it's a bit suspicious.

SPIORAD
I'm being awfully patient with you, human female. You could at the *very least* entertain the idea a bit.

AMANDA
I *am* entertaining the idea. I find it *very* entertaining.

SPIORAD
If you're going to give me sass, I'll just get up and leave.

AMANDA
What a *horrible* tragedy that will be.

SPIORAD
I know the way out of the woods.

A pause as AMANDA thinks about this.

SPIORAD
(Mostly to himself. In a sing-song voice) Travellers lost in the woods without sight of the path. Travellers lost without hope or recognition.

AMANDA
What the heck are you talking about?

SPIORAD
Travellers lost in the shadows. Without hope or recognition.

AMANDA
Spiorad-

SPIORAD
Lost in the woods until they once again reach the moor.

SPIORAD *(cont.)*
My job is to lead the lost back to the path. But I haven't talked with anyone in a while. So I'm going to put a price on my services.

AMANDA
That sounds really weird.

SPIORAD
Tell me your story. Give me a reason to lead you from the woods. I'll be fair, I'll tell you mine once you're done.

AMANDA
Why can't you just be nice and show me the way out?

SPIORAD
I am a Nature Spirit. This is what I do.

       AMANDA sticks her tongue out at him, but sighs and simply shrugs
AMANDA
Well, what do I say, 'Mr. Nature Spirit?' I'm a girl with a history of bad luck.

SPIORAD
(Gently) Bad luck has no meaning in the woods.

AMANDA
(Softly) I.... I had a good life. I lived with my parents in a nice neighborhood. I had friends. I did well in school.

    SPIORAD tilts his head at the word 'school,' but stays silent.

AMANDA *(cont.)*
A house full of love. That's what I had. A family that cared for each other.

SPIORAD
(To himself) A family...

AMANDA
I was a stupid little kid. I thought that I was going to be happy forever. I never saw it coming. I didn't expect to see the men at my door who took me away. In truth, it was all sort of a haze. It's weird when

someone tells you that your parents are dead. Your whole body goes cold... like you've just plunged yourself into deep snow. Then there's a jolt. A horrible jolt in the bottom of your stomach.

SPIORAD
I know.

AMANDA
(Surprised) What?

SPIORAD
(Wearily) You don't see anyone else around, do you? I'm alone. All alone.

AMANDA
(More gentle) I... I didn't realize...

SPIORAD
(To himself) It's a funny thing, losing someone. You forget to talk to people. You think that your life is ending.

AMANDA
After a few days, everyone expects you to get over it. It's an old story. It's the past.

SPIORAD
No one understands.

AMANDA
Not unless they know.

> *A long pause. SPIORAD and AMANDA stare at each other for a moment.*

SPIORAD
(To himself) Travellers lost in the woods tell me their stories. In return, I show them the way.

AMANDA
You promised you'd tell me *your* story.

SPIORAD
My story is your story.

AMANDA
(With a small laugh) I doubt that it's *exactly* the same.

> *SPIORAD hesitates.*

SPIORAD
I didn't have a house, but I had a family. A family that cared. They were all I needed. They were all that really mattered.

AMANDA
So your story *is* different.

SPIORAD
The plot is the same. I had a family. I lost it. I was alone.

AMANDA
What happened?

> *SPIORAD is silent.*

AMANDA *(cont.)*
I told you what happened to *me*. I think it's only fair.

> *SPIORAD is silent.*

AMANDA *(cont.)*
We have to start somewhere.

SPIORAD
(Bitterly) What happened to them was no accident. My survival was not a blessing, but a punishment. I am alone to walk the woods, bound by grief and guilt.

AMANDA
(Understanding) Guilt.

SPIORAD
I should have died with them.

AMANDA
Guilt.

SPIORAD
The details are not important.

AMANDA
I understand how you're feeling.

SPIORAD
(Surprised) What?

> *AMANDA gives a reassuring smile.*

AMANDA
Maybe we can both help each other find the path again.

SPIORAD
(Confused) I know these woods already.

AMANDA
Something more than the woods.

A long pause. SPIORAD stands up and offers his hand.

SPIORAD
I'm not one to say this to a human... but... maybe I'll let you.

AMANDA
Then we're gonna have to get to know each other.

SPIORAD
You've already told me your story.

AMANDA
Life isn't just one story.

SPIORAD
(With a soft chuckle) I guess that's true.

AMANDA
(Demanding) Now show me the way.

SPIORAD
(Cheeky) I have a feeling that you'll be coming back.

AMANDA
Wait and see, 'Mr. Nature Spirit.'
Hand in hand, the two walk offstage.

Scene 5:
At rise, O'CONNOR is sitting on the porch, smoking a pipe. He is mumbling a tune under his breath.
AMANDA walks in, putting her hair up.

O'CONNOR
Where do you think *you're* going, lassie?

AMANDA
Exploring the woods.

O'CONNOR
(Suspiciously) You've been going out there a lot... ever since that one time a few days ago-

AMANDA
Grandpa O'Connor, are you telling me that I can't go exploring? That I can't let the 'magic of this place' heal me?

O'CONNOR

I never said that. I'm just worried.

Slight pause

AMANDA
Grandpa, what are Nature Spirits?

O'CONNOR
(Shocked) W- what?

AMANDA
Nature Spirits.

O'CONNOR
Amanda, what are you doing in the woods?

AMANDA
I'm just asking a question! I thought you knew all about these things!

O'CONNOR
I do, I just want to make sure that you're not-

AMANDA sits down and faces him

AMANDA
Tell me.

O'CONNOR
(Hesitant) Now look... I know how you feel about the whole 'magic thing.' If this is your way of making *fun* of me-

AMANDA
Grandpa!

O'CONNOR
Alright, alright... what was your question?

AMANDA
What are Nature Spirits?

O'CONNOR
Ah.... um, well that's a tough one, lassie.

AMANDA
Why?

O'CONNOR
They're pretty mysterious. Not seen often.

AMANDA
What do they do? Are they ghosts?

O'CONNOR
Ack! Calm yourself! No, they're not, from what I've heard. They're.... protectors of nature. They punish those that disrespect the wild... Cause mischief... There aren't many stories, Amanda.

AMANDA
That's too bad.

O'CONNOR
Why are you asking this?

AMANDA
(Standing) No reason. Just wondering. Well, I'd better be off.

        She begins to walk away, but O'CONNOR reaches out and grabs her wrist.
O'CONNOR
Be careful, alright?

AMANDA
(Brightly) Of course! Thanks grandpa!

She kisses his cheek and runs off. O'CONNOR smiles after her for a moment, but then frowns suspiciously again and looks off towards the woods.
After a moment of thought, he follows her.

Scene 6:
At rise, AMANDA walks onstage hesitantly, looking up at the branches overhead.

AMANDA
Spiorad! Spiorad! Are you here?

        SPIORAD enters behind her, silent. AMANDA doesn't notice.

AMANDA
Spiorad!

SPIORAD
(Softly) Boo.

AMANDA
GAH! What the heck?!?

SPIORAD
I got you. You said you weren't going to fall for that anymore.

AMANDA

I forgot! Besides, Nature Spirits can walk so unnaturally quiet!

SPIORAD
(Pleased) Ah, so you *do* believe me now!

AMANDA
I guess I have no other choice.

SPIORAD
It only took you *four* days.

AMANDA
Well, I'm *sorry!* It was just a little creepy at the start is all.

SPIORAD
Creepy? Excuse me.

AMANDA
Sorry. I forgot you don't like that word.

SPIORAD
It's alright. If you call me creepy, I'll just call you weird.

AMANDA
(Sarcastically) Ha, ha... funny, Spiorad.

SPIORAD
So, Mr. O'Connor is starting to suspect something, huh?

AMANDA
(Startled) What? How would you-

Short pause.

AMANDA *(cont.)*
You don't look through my WINDOW, do you?

SPIORAD
(Flabbergasted) No, of course not!

AMANDA
Just checking.

SPIORAD
You're gonna have to be careful. O'Connor won't like you hanging around a Nature Spirit.

AMANDA
I will be careful. Don't you worry.

SPIORAD and AMANDA sit on the floor.

SPIORAD
What's bothering you?

AMANDA
I'm just... thinking about what's going to happen to me. After I leave.

SPIORAD
You'll go on with your life, I suppose.

AMANDA
But I won't be able to. That's the point. My parents were everything; they told me what to wear, what to eat, where to go...

SPIORAD
It's a big jump, I know, but you'll learn how to do those things yourself.

AMANDA
I don't want to learn how to do those things myself. I want my parents to nag at me again, and I want to be annoyed with them.

SPIORAD
You *want* to be annoyed?

AMANDA
Hmph, other people don't understand! You wouldn't get it either!
Short pause.

SPIORAD
(Slowly) There was once a boy that lived in the woods.

AMANDA
(Surprised/Confused) What are you talking about?

SPIORAD
This little boy was young and naive. He frolicked and played, without a care in the whole world.

He pauses for a short moment, as if debating whether to go on.

SPIORAD *(cont.)*
And this little boy had a family; a mother and a father. And he loved them with all his heart. And they loved him back. Everything was happy. Everything was fine.

AMANDA
Spiorad-

SPIORAD
One day, when he was walking in the woods, this little boy heard a sound echoing through the trees. It was loud and sharp, almost a pop. This was followed by a scream.

A short pause.

SPIORAD *(cont.)*
The little boy ran and ran, too scared to know what was going on. He wanted to get away from the noise and the screaming. He wanted to get far, far away.

(As the story continues, SPIORAD should sound more and more like he's about to cry)

SPIORAD *(cont.)*
He hid in a log, trembling and frightened. He heard noises outside, like the thundering of footsteps and the shouting of men. But he was frightened, so he hid. When... when the noises stopped... the little boy crawled out and went looking for his parents. He called out to them. He went to where he had seen them last and begged them to stop hiding. There were no more sounds. They could stop hiding.

SPIORAD pauses for a moment. AMANDA looks uncomfortable, but is hypnotized by the tale.

SPIORAD *(cont.)*
He searched for two days. And then it became clear that his family wasn't going to come back. At first, he hoped that he could follow them, wherever they were, but... after a few more days...

SPIORAD shakes his head. AMANDA places a hand on his shoulder.

AMANDA
Spiorad...

SPIORAD
I felt broken inside. I never realized how fragile I was until then. I couldn't do anything but sit in the rain, staring at the ground, wondering what had happened to me... I thought I was going to rot away on the floor and die along with my happiness. Sound familiar to you?

AMANDA looks like she's about to cry

SPIORAD
I am someone who had my world taken away. And I am someone who survived.

AMANDA
I.... Spiorad... My grandpa wouldn't-

SPIORAD
It wasn't him. It was someone else. But take advice from someone who understands. It's painful, but in their memory you have to go on. They wouldn't want you to die along with them. They made you. They want you to carry on their story. Be happy, if not for yourself, then for them.

AMANDA
I don't know if-.... should I just-..... I'll try...

SPIORAD
Don't try. Do it. Be brave for yourself and the people you have left.

AMANDA reacts to his words.

AMANDA
Brave. Like... mom.

SPIORAD takes her hand and gives it a squeeze.

SPIORAD
In my language, there's a word. *Rúnda.*

AMANDA
Rúnda.
SPIORAD
It means friend. It is friends that can help drag you from the darkness and help you find the light. Friends that understand.

AMANDA
Rúnda.

SPIORAD
You are my friend. Let me lead you to the light.

AMANDA
(Teasing) It's your job to help those who are lost to find the path again, huh?

SPIORAD
Let one who knows your pain help you.

Short pause.

AMANDA
Rúnda... I like that. It's pretty.

SPIORAD
Rúnda. Yes, it *is* pretty.

AMANDA
You'll be my friend?

SPIORAD
(With a laugh) I *am* your friend, silly.

AMANDA
That makes me feel better.

Pause.

AMANDA
Oh crap! The sun! I promised Grandpa that I'd be home before the sun sets!

SPIORAD
(With a snicker) You know the way. It won't take long. Unless you've forgotten, of course.
They both stand up. AMANDA hesitates.
She leans over and hugs SPIORAD tightly. He is confused at first, but returns the embrace.
They pull away.

AMANDA
Thank you. For listening.

SPIORAD
Yes. I would say the same thing, but then it would seem like I'm copying you.

AMANDA laughs. They both exit.

Scene 7:
At rise, O'Connor is seated at the kitchen table, hunched over. Amanda runs in, out of breath and smiling.

AMANDA
Hey grandpa! Sorry I'm late! I lost track of time, and I just-

O'CONNOR
(Almost a whisper) How could you?

Pause

AMANDA
(Confused) Grandpa?

O'CONNOR
I followed you.

A pause.

O'CONNOR *(cont.)*
I thought I told you to be careful.

AMANDA
I *am* being careful!

O'CONNOR
(Furious) I warned you! I *warned* you! But then you just go out and walk in the woods, getting yourself lost in the trees-

AMANDA

Grandpa-

O'CONNOR
I spent an *hour* looking for you-

AMANDA
Grandpa!

O'CONNOR
And when I *do* find you, you're getting *seduced* by a demon!

AMANDA
(Sputtering) Excuse me?!?

O'CONNOR
You careless brat! I *warned* you to be careful! Do you *know* what those things do!? Those creatures are *monsters!*

AMANDA
Spiorad isn't like that! You've got it wrong.

O'CONNOR!
Enough! Enough! I know what's best for you! I will not allow a monster to take the only thing I have left!

AMANDA
(Tries to grab O'CONNOR'S arm) Stop it! Stop it! You've got it all wrong! He isn't-

O'CONNOR
(Shakes her off forcefully) I will deal with this! I should have finished that thing the minute I knew it was there! That *monster!* That creature of *destruction!*

AMANDA
(Pleading/Almost sobbing) Grandpa! Stop it!
O'CONNOR
I won't let it take you away!

O'CONNOR, despite AMANDA'S screaming, runs offstage. AMANDA staggers around for a moment, not fully realizing what's happening.

AMANDA
He... Oh god, he's going to *kill* him!

She chases after O'CONNOR.

AMANDA (O.S)
Spiorad! Spiorad!

Scene 8:
At rise, AMANDA runs onstage, out of breath.

AMANDA
(Almost screaming) Spiorad!

SPIORAD runs onstage, looking startled

SPIORAD
Amanda? What's the matter-?

AMANDA
(Sobbing) Spiorad!

She runs to him and grabs his arm.

AMANDA (cont.)
(In a broken voice) Y- you have to get away!! Gr- Grandpa!

SPIORAD
(Confused/Spooked) What's happening?

AMANDA
Gr-grandpa! He knows! He- he's gone crazy! He knows about you!
SPIORAD
That's nothing new.

AMANDA
(Desperate) You don't understand!! He's looking for you! I- he's going to kill you!

SPIORAD is just beginning to grasp the situation.

SPIORAD
What should I-

O'CONNOR enters.

O'CONNOR
Get away from her, you scum!

AMANDA
Grandpa! No! Stop it!

O'CONNOR
Amanda, get away from it! Get away from it now!

AMANDA
Stop it! He's not dangerous!

O'CONNOR

I SAID GET AWAY!

O'CONNOR lungs at the two, grabbing SPIORAD by the shoulder and digging in with his fingernails. AMANDA is tossed to the side.

AMANDA
(Screaming) GRANDPA! NO! DON'T HURT HIM!!

SPIORAD clenches his teeth, but makes no move to protect himself. O'CONNOR tries to take him by the throat.

O'CONNOR
I won't lose you! Not you! You're all I have left! Maria-!

AMANDA tries to pry O'CONNOR'S fingers off of SPIORAD'S neck.

AMANDA
LEAVE HIM ALONE! HE'S MY FRIEND!

She managed to pull the two apart. AMANDA then stands in front of SPIORAD protectively.

O'CONNOR
Get away from it!

AMANDA
(In a quivering but loud voice) Rúnda!

O'CONNOR freezes.

SPIORAD
(Painfully) What are you doing?

AMANDA
(To O'CONNOR) Friend.

A long pause. O'CONNOR stares at the two. AMANDA does not budge.

O'CONNOR
(Pleading) Amanda....

AMANDA does not answer

O'CONNOR *(cont.)*
Please...

AMANDA is silent. O'CONNOR suddenly bursts into tears.

O'CONNOR

I can't lose you! I can't kill you like I did to Maria!

AMANDA is obviously disturbed by this. She takes a few hesitant steps towards her grandfather.

O'CONNOR
(Hysterical) I killed her! I killed her! She left because she wanted freedom from me!

AMANDA
(Kneels in front of O'CONNOR) You didn't kill her! It was an accident! An *accident!*

O'CONNOR
(Weakly) I can't lose you too. I have to save you...

AMANDA hugs her grandfather. SPIORAD remains where he is, motionless.

AMANDA
You *did* save me. Grandpa, you *have* saved me.

O'CONNOR
(Returning the hug) Maria...

AMANDA
Grandpa, coming here has healed me, just like you said it would.

O'CONNOR
I killed Maria.

AMANDA
It wasn't your fault. It wasn't my fault. It wasn't *anyone's* fault. She died. Grandpa, it was an accident. An *accident!*

O'CONNOR
... Amanda.

AMANDA
Grandpa.

O'CONNOR
Amanda. I love you.

O'CONNOR pulls her into a tighter hug. SPIORAD silently leaves, casting a quick glance over his shoulder. Neither AMANDA nor O'CONNOR notices.

O'CONNOR
I love you so much.... lassie...

AMANDA
I love you too, grandpa....

AMANDA puts O'CONNOR's arm around her shoulders and stands up.

AMANDA
Let's go home.

O'CONNOR
Amanda....

AMANDA looks behind her and sees that SPIORAD is no longer there. She hesitates for a moment, but helps her grandfather offstage.

Scene 9:
At rise, O'CONNOR is seated on the porch. Amanda walks onstage with a glass of water. Wearily, O'CONNOR accepts the beverage.

O'CONNOR
Thank you lassie...

AMANDA
You're welcome.

She sits next to him and looks off into the woods longingly.

O'CONNOR
(Guilty) You want to go check on him, don't you?

AMANDA
I... want to make sure he's okay... but I can stay with you, if you want.

O'CONNOR
(Apologetic) I'm sorry. I was a fool but... I didn't... want to hurt you. I let my emotions cloud my judgement.

AMANDA
It's alright. I know how that feels.

O'CONNOR
You're all I have left, lassie. You know that.

AMANDA
Yeah...

A short pause.

O'CONNOR
(Thoughtfully) Rúnda...

AMANDA
What?

O'CONNOR
You said that yesterday. In the woods. Rúnda.

AMANDA
(Almost smiling) Yes. It means friend.

O'CONNOR
Friend.

AMANDA
He understands. He listens.

O'CONNOR
I listen.

AMANDA
I know you do, grandpa... it's just... hearing someone else comfort me in the way he did... I dunno. It felt...
different.
O'CONNOR
(Smiling/To himself) Such is the silver tongue of a Nature Spirit.

AMANDA
(After a moment) Would mom have done what I did?

O'CONNOR
Your mother had an energetic, caring soul. Yes, she probably would have done the same things you did.
She knew right and wrong better than me. I am an old fool.

AMANDA
You were just doing what you thought was right.

A pause.

O'CONNOR
Did your mother ever tell you *why* she left?

AMANDA
(Confused) No... was there a reason?

O'CONNOR
(With a sigh) I was a bit controlling, I'll admit. My only daughter. My life, after your grandmother died,
was all about Maria. She was my angel. My only. When she met your father and wanted to go see the
world... I was selfish. I tried to force her to stay. But it didn't work out the way I thought it would... and I
only succeeded in pushing her farther away from me. She walked out of my life forever. The next time
that I saw her... she was independent. A different Maria.

A short pause.

O'CONNOR *(cont.)*
I'm glad you're here, lassie.

AMANDA
I'm glad I came.

O'CONNOR
Go on. Go look for that Irish Spirit of yours. He's probably watching anyway. He tends to do that.

AMANDA hesitates

O'CONNOR *(cont.)*
Oh, I'll survive. I have to learn to let go. As long as I know you'll come back to me, I don't mind sharing.

AMANDA
Thank you grandpa.

She leans over and kisses O'CONNOR on the cheek.

AMANDA *(cont.)*
And don't worry. I won't leave you all alone.

She runs offstage. O'CONNOR sighs and glances at his water glass.

O'CONNOR
What a sweet girl.... to care about an old fool like me.

He sets down the glass and leans back in his chair.

O'CONNOR *(cont.)*
What a sweet girl...

A pause

O'CONNOR *(cont.)*
Just like you....

He smiles to himself and sighs.

O'CONNOR *(cont.)*
... Maria.

END OF PLAY

Nomads Theatre Company , UCSD
& High Tech High North County, San Marcos

A collaboration: New plays written by high school students and brought to life by college students and recent college graduates

Below is the list of these original plays' original actors.

1. The Chit Chat Game by Liana Goldberg
Chad: Elliott Beltran   Sarah: Susannah Snowden-Ifft
What if Sarah & Chad struggle to connect in real life after connecting online?

2. The Dragon's Egg by Megan Lambert (10th)
Princess Tiffany: Devon Hollingsworth   Prince Titus: Edward Delos Reyes   Benedict Cumberbatch: Jethro Antonio
What if the princess doesn't want to be saved by the prince?

3. Finding a Cure by Ramon Solis (12th)
Jason: Jethro Antonio   Jackson: Elliott Beltran   Julia: Stacy Mauro
What if a man was on the brink of death and his brother had the intellectual capability to find a cure?

4. Photosynthesis by Anna Ryburn (9th)
Leon: Edward Delos Reyes   Ashley: Stacy Mauro   Narissa: Victoria Le
What if your plant decided to one day become human?

5. Together, Selfless by Sydney Luke-Hamasaki (11th)
Reed: Devon Hollingsworth   Blade: Elliott Beltran   Ana-Mia: Victoria Le
What if the people around you weren't exactly who you thought they were?

6. The Chameleon Project by Natasha Oslinger (9th)
Willow: Victoria Le Aiden: Stacy Mauro
What if you could create an extension of yourself?

7. Runda by Gabriela Schnepp (9th)
Amanda: Susannah Snowden-Ifft   O'Connor: Edward Delos Reyes   Spiorad: Elliott Beltran
What if a girl connected with her heritage after losing her family in a car accident?

8. The Rebels by Nathan Smith (12th)
Carl: Jethro Antonio   Rex: Edward Delos Reyes
What if a soldier and his captain were from different planets and were on a mission in space?

9. Perfectly Sane by Skylar Rees (9th)
Seth: Elliott Beltran   Lilly: Susannah Snowden-Ifft   Raelyn: Devon Hollingsworth
What if three people in a facility found a way to share their stories with one another?

Nomads Theatre Company could not do the work they do without the generous donations of their wonderful audiences. Please consider donating to Nomads Theatre Company today.
www.nomadstheatrecompany.com

The objective behind Nomads Theatre Company has always been to provide a means to develop the theatrical artist, to provide a voice to otherwise untapped potential. In the span of a year, we have seen work from all over the country be produced through Nomads. Playwrights of all ages have submitted work to us, but it is always exciting to work with the younger generation--our core. What Carol is providing through this writing intensive is a wonderful example of how we can foster creativity in our students and keep art alive in our schools. I am glad to be a part of it.

~Edward Delos Reyes, Artistic Director, Nomads Theatre Company 2014

Stacey Mauro (left) with Natasha Oslinger (playwright) and Vicky Tran (left).

Elliot Beltran (left) with Skylar Haynes (playwright), Susannah Snowden-Ifft and Devon Hollingsworth

A Note from Carol

I cannot remember a time in my life where I did not identify as an artist. And when I turned teacher, I had a bit of a time trying to balance my two selves, until I realized that the two could be one in the same--that as an artist, I could support the inner artists in every one of my students.

I am so lucky to work in an environment where everyone is interested in hearing student voices and in pushing students to expand their horizons and stretch their imaginations. This collection of plays was written in one week in my classroom, 129 at High Tech High North County in a sometimes very formal, sometimes very lab-like writing structure.

I must thank Isaac Jones, and all of High Tech High North County's very supportive faculty and staff. Thanks to the wonderful parents of these fantastic, creative writers. Gratitude to California Playwright's Project, the organization who gave me my love of playwriting. More thanks to Tim West of Cygnet Theatre Company, who came out to talk to students about their ideas and provide more ways to reach inside to find really honest, thought-provoking writing.

A very special thanks to Edward Delos Reyes & Nomads Theatre Company for continuously supporting me, my students and the work that I love. This collection of plays is of a very diverse selection, and I hope that you can find a story that resonates with you, connects with you, is you somewhere in these pieces.

Love,
Carol Cabrera

PS. I'm always looking for feedback as a teacher. I want to be the best teacher I can possibly be for every learner that walks through my door. So if you have any feedback for me or if you have any comments or any other conversation to have with me, please email me! mscarolcabrera@gmail.com

www.ingramcontent.com/pod-product-compliance
Lightning Source LLC
Chambersburg PA
CBHW050947030426
42339CB00007B/321